LAZARIS

LAZARIS INTERVIEWS BOOK I

CONCEPT: SYNERGY PUBLISHING

Who is Lazaris?

Lazaris is a non-physical entity. He is a consciousness without form — a Spark of Light, a Spark of Love — an energy that has never chosen to take human form. He is most frequently known as "the one who waits for us at the edge of our reality."

Lazaris is wise beyond what we have known, loving beyond what we have conceived, and committed to each of us in our search for enlightenment. He is a delightful friend — a gentle and powerful guide for our Spiritual Journey Home to God/Goddess/All That Is.

The way that Lazaris communicates to us is called channeling — in this case Objective, Full-Trance Channeling. That means several things. "Objective" means that Lazaris is not a part of the consciousness of his channel. "Full Trance" means that the channel (Jach Pursel) is not aware of what is being said during the trance state. "Channeling" is perhaps best described by Lazaris directly:

"In order to communicate with you, we send forth a series of vibrations. These vibratory frequencies go through a series of 'step-down generations' until they can safely enter your reality.

"The energy field of the one you call Jach acts like an antenna; his body, like an amplifier. The vibration we create in our reality is thus amplified in your reality. Your ears and eyes pick up those amplified frequencies and translate them into sounds — you hear a voice — and pictures — you see animation.

"When we communicate we are not in the body — how archaic! Such behavior is no more necessary than having your nightly newscaster actually be in your television set!

"We keep the channel in a sleep-like state so that he stays out of the way. It would be possible for him to 'witness' what we say — to 'listen' as the vibrations go by — but we prefer him to be completely out of the way. The best way to keep the information pure is to have the channel be as much a 'pure instrument' as possible."

Lazaris is a channeled entity, but he is so very much more. Many who are familiar with metaphysics and channeling say, "There is channeling, and then there is Lazaris. He is so far beyond ... he stands alone in this field."

Lazaris...

Lazaris says he came not as a guru, but as a friend. I've found that what I value most I've learned from friends, and Lazaris is one of the best friends I have.

— *Colin Higgins, Writer/Director, "Harold & Maude," "Silver Streak," "Foul Play," "The Best Little Whorehouse in Texas," "Nine to Five"*

Lazaris represents the Highest Self of humanity. When one is in communication with him it activates that Highest Self in that person. Lazaris' energy literally magnetizes that Highest Self to be experienced as real, as who we really are. It is a privilege and vital opportunity to communicate with this level of consciousness.

— *Barbara Marx Hubbard, Futurist*

Lazaris is the friend we always wish for, and now he's here for everyone. We had a good relationship before, but he showed us how to love each other even more. We always thought that success came after long and hard work. Lazaris taught us it's more fun to do it quicker and easier. With Lazaris' love and help we have created one miracle after another.

— *Renée Taylor & Joe Bologna, Actors, Writers & Directors*

With wisdom, compassion and marvelous humor, Lazaris, from his greater perspective outside our "Set," makes vividly clear how physical reality works. He knows me absolutely and is there for me — even when I am not! Thank you, Lazaris. I love you. . . .

— *Betty Fuller, Director, The Trager Institute*

I went to Lazaris' first public channeling in 1979. Since that day the quality of information and communication has always expanded and surpassed itself. The growth I have made because of our friendship has brought me into the New Age with clarity and assurance. I love Lazaris even more today and rejoice in our shared vision for the exciting future!

— *Nicholas Eliopoulos, Producer/Director/Writer, and Emmy Award-winning Editor for "Wallenberg: A Hero's Story," Senior Vice President of Development/ Production, The Don Johnson Company*

Lazaris, it's magic! It is magic! Thank you, Lazaris, for showing me how to pull rabbits out of hats!

—*Sharon Gless, "Cagney & Lacey"*

LAZARIS

LAZARIS INTERVIEWS
BOOK I

CONCEPT: SYNERGY PUBLISHING

Lazaris

Lazaris Interviews, Book I

1st Printing, 1988
© *1988 Concept: Synergy Publishing, 279 S. Beverly Drive, Suite 604,*
Beverly Hills, CA 90212, 213/285-1507
Cover photograph by Michaell North
ISBN 1-55638-072-2, Library of Congress Catalog Card Number 88-070670
Printed in the United States of America
10 9 8 7 6 5 4 3 2 1

Dedication

This book is dedicated to Peny,
the one we came to touch,
the one who truly touches us.
We love you.

—Lazaris

Books by Lazaris

A Note on Lazaris' Use of Language ...

Throughout this book Lazaris refers to himself as "we." Ever since he began communicating with us in 1974, he has done that. Lazaris says that each of us has many "selves," but that right now we are experiencing them "one at a time," and thus refer to ourselves as "I". Lazaris has many selves as well — many selves in many dimensions — but experiences them all simultaneously, and therefore refers to himself as "we". It is not the use of the "royal we," but rather Lazaris' experience of his own reality. ...

Also, often you will find that Lazaris will use a plural pronoun in a place you might expect to find a singular one. This is to avoid using the generic masculine pronouns which tend to make women feel as though they are not included in what is being said. To make certain they do know they are included, Lazaris often uses plural pronouns which, though "against the rules," are better aligned with what is true.

Contents

Acknowledgements

This book is made up of a number of interviews, and in addition incorporates the questions and answers from the Evenings with Lazaris which have followed Weekends with Lazaris (two-day seminars). Following each question is a line that identifies the publication and the interviewer who asked the question — or the workshop at which the question was asked. In the case where there are several consecutive questions from the same interview, the identifying line follows the answer to the last question in the series.

Lazaris and Concept: Synergy gratefully acknowledge and thank the following people and publications for their participation in generating the material for this book:

Alan Vaughan, *Whole Life Monthly*, 409 Santa Monica Blvd., Suite 212, Santa Monica, California 90401.

Brian Enright and Lisa Michelle Guest, *Los Angeles and Orange County Resources*, published by Community Resource Publications, 228 Twentieth Street, Huntington Beach, CA 92648.

Craig Lee, *LA Weekly*, 2140 Hyperion Avenue, Los Angeles, CA 90027, used by permission.

David Rogers, *Llewellyn's New Times*, 213 E. Fourth Street, St. Paul, Minnesota, 55101.

Lee Perry, 17510 Sherman Way, #212, Van Nuys, California, 91406.

Mary Ellen Pratt and Jack Clarke, *New Age Information Network*, P. O. Box 566714, Atlanta, Georgia, 30356.

Penny Price, *A Complete Guide to Channeling* (video), Penny Price Productions, 670 El Media Avenue, Pacific Palisades, California, 90272, used by permission.

Krysta Gibson, *The New Times & The Spiritual Women's Times*, P. O. Box 51186, Seattle, Washington 98115-1186.

Cindy Saul, *PhenomeNEWS*, 28545 Greenfield, Suite 111, Southfield, Michigan 48076.

E. James Faubel, *Transformation Times*, P. O. Box 425, Beaver Creek, Oregon 97004.

Marilyn Ferguson, *Brain/Mind Bulletin*, P. O. Box 42211, Los Angeles, California 90042.

Louise L. Hay, Hay House, Inc., 501 Santa Monica Blvd., Suite 602, Santa Monica, California 90401.

Van Ault, *Magical Blend Magazine*, P. O. Box 11303, San Francisco, California 94101.

Merv Griffin, *The Merv Griffin Show*, by permission of Merv Griffin Enterprises, 1541 N. Vine Street, Hollywood, California 90028.

The participants of the Seattle and Atlanta Evenings with Lazaris, and the Los Angeles Whole Life Expo 1987, at which Lazaris spoke, who asked anonymous questions that became a part of this book.

We would also like to thank Michaell North for his cover photograph of Lazaris and Norman Seeff for the photographs of Lazaris and Jach Pursel that are found in the body of this book.

A special thank you to Zoë Landers and Morgaan Sinclair for their valuable and consistent help in putting this book together.

Introductions

Introduction by Jach Pursel — From Lazaris — From Peny

Introduction

by Jach Pursel

I still remember the first meditation. The path twisted this way and that. Green ... everything so very green. The ferns, tall. Trees, lush. Sweet smells. So engrossed in the detail, I forgot to be startled. I forgot to disbelieve.

The images burst. My mind raced ahead. I kept following. Then I saw an intriguing cabin. "Oh, brother," I thought. "This is just too corny! This is almost embarrassing!" But there was something different about this particular cabin. The spontaneity and the uniqueness silenced my skepticism and my sarcasm.

Surrounded in tall pines and sequoias, it had a thatched roof and sparkling glass windows with diamond-shaped beveled panes. The exterior walls were rough cut, but the slightly ajar door was smooth and finely crafted. It was certainly "Americana," but it was something else as well. It intrigued me. It welcomed me.

Maybe it was the twill of smoke. Perhaps it was the warmth of the light pouring from windows and door. The details astonished me. The racing stopped.

I stood for a very long time. Inching my way, the path gave way to three steps. I finally crossed the porch and reached for the latch. The door opened on its own. My skepticism bubbled briefly. I could almost hear it breathe. I stepped into the room.

A man was standing in front of me. He was gentle. I was not afraid. He spoke to me. I remembered every word. Our relationship began ...

Now, so many years later, I see Lazaris as the spark of love and light that he more correctly is. When I need answers to specific questions, I give Peny a list and she records or notes the responses during her next private time with Lazaris.

Sometimes I need the feeling of Lazaris more than the facts of his answers. When I want to just be with Lazaris, I return to that "almost embarrassing," but very real, place. Each time, I repeat the steps. Each time, I reach for the latch and the door opens by itself. Each time.

Lazaris is always there for me. He is always there. During these feeling times, I don't ask anything. I sit with Lazaris. His energy envelopes me. I let him embrace me with his love, his caring, and his intimacy. I experience his compassion. I experience beyond the words that he might speak. I experience Lazaris.

I needed one of those feeling times when Lazaris decided to make video tapes. Prior to November, 1986, Lazaris had been talking with people privately and conducting afternoon workshops and weekend seminars. Though there were many thousands of people who participated in the consultations and the events, my experience of it all was still very personal and very private.

The release of video tapes and making the audio tapes available through bookstores and centers throughout the United States, Canada, Australia, and selected places in Europe and Asia, seemed too public — too visible. I sat with Lazaris. I stretched my image. I let in a little more of who Lazaris is and what he's about. I let him in. It became okay.

As I learn and grow with Lazaris — I listen to the tapes and take notes just like everyone else — those feeling times have become increasingly important. I sit with Lazaris for what seems like forever. Well, a very long time, at least. Then a rush of insight explodes inside of me. Gestalts seem to unfold spontaneously like fireworks on the Fourth of July. As abruptly, the experience ends. My eyes open. I have the sense of knowing. It's wonderful.

When it came time to decide whether to compile and release *Lazaris Interviews*, I needed one of those feeling times. Quite frankly, I had reservations.

Interview questions and answers are never intended to be a definitive exploration and explanation of a topic. The questions are pointed, and the answers are brief. What Lazaris would say to this question or that would not be his complete and total answer. Would people understand that? Would people mistakenly think this was all Lazaris had to say on a particular topic or issue? Would it be better to wait until Lazaris presented a fuller picture in a future book?

Due to the time/space considerations of the interview format, Lazaris answered questions as succinctly as possible. Would people mistake his brevity for shallowness?

When Lazaris does a workshop, he responds to the energy — the needs and wants — of the participants. When he responds to an interviewer, he answers in such a way that the questioner and audience will best understand — will best be able to relate to — what he's saying. How will regional questions and answers translate to a universal readership?

Many interviews ask the same questions. How can we keep the book from being redundant and still retain the integrity of each interview?

My mind raced with resistance. What format? Is it organized by interview or by topic? How do we decide which questions to include and which ones to leave out? How do we decide which repeated question goes in and which goes out? How ...? I was on a roll!

Finally I stopped and went to the feeling place with Lazaris. I sat. Oh, I wanted to argue and resolve all my "what if's" and "how about's." I sat. I let Lazaris in. I let him love me. In his way he told me: "Read it. Just read it."

That was it. Nothing profound. Or at least nothing that seemed profound at the time.

As the pieces of the books were fitted together, I began to read. It was very late one night — I tend to stay up very late since I spend so much time in trance. I run off the energy at three or four in the morning. I make up for the hours I spend in trance late at night when everyone else is sleeping. I began to read.

As I am reading, my mind flashes on that one evening back in 1976. It was very late then, too. I was all alone like I am now. The room was totally dark. Well, it's almost like that now. Then I was listening to a cassette tape; now I'm reading.

I remember. I was lying on the floor just listening. I was still amazed that that voice was coming out of my body. Now I am more used to it, though not totally. That night I just listened.

That night I heard the words, but I heard something more. It was something between the words. It was in the timbre, the cadence. It was in the urgency and the patience. I heard the love. That night, all alone, I heard the caring, the intimacy that Lazaris feels for each of us — for all of us. I heard the compassion.

Gripping the pages of manuscript, the same feeling washed over me. Tears once again rolled down my face. The tears gave way to sobs. Once again, I could feel Lazaris filling me with his incredible love and his soothing peace. I understood.

I could feel Lazaris in each answer I was reading, of course. More than that, I could feel Lazaris between the words. I could feel him in the style of response. I could feel him in each "we suggest" and in each "in that particular regard."

More importantly, people would feel that, too. Yes, the interviews would be read for information. More, the interviews would be read for their feeling and the understanding. The interviews would be read for the love, the light, the laughter, and the joy that is Lazaris.

Now I know why Lazaris said: "Read it. Just read it."

Enjoy for yourself. Let yourself learn. Let yourself experience the "feeling" time with Lazaris.

Jach Pursel
Los Angeles, March, 1988

From Lazaris ...

Well, all right. It is a pleasure to be working with you — it is a pleasure to be writing to you. Our purpose in communicating — in channeling our information — has been stated frequently. The media, many times intent upon being critical, has actually contributed to the dissemination of information more than it would like to admit.

You as individuals, as society, and as a humanity have decided to accelerate your growth and expand your awareness. You have asked for help.

More than ever, you are creating a Rubik's Cube-like reality where it seems like any one solution only leads to several more problems. The old answers born of linear problem solving simply do not work anymore. You have asked for new answers.

Our way of helping — our way of offering new answers — is to provide you with opportunity. Through exploration and examination we want to provide you the opportunity to encounter, unfold, befriend, and change your reality. We want to show you your actual old forms of reality creation and your potential new forms of future manifestation. We want to show you how to bridge from old to new.

If what you find in your exploration is detrimental, then we want to show you how to transmute and transform that energy into a power you can use to create a happier, more successful reality for yourself. We want to show you how to create a happier, more successful future for yourself and your world.

If what you discover augments who you are, we want to show you how to lift that awareness of self to a level of self-realization that can have a more profound, a more far-reaching impact upon you, your reality, and your future world.

With all the private consultations and workshop discussions, with all the meditations and Blendings, and with all the audio and video tapes, one of the common denominators is to consistently and continuously offer you the opportunity. Your opportunity.

Another common denominator is to offer you these opportunities via the means, the powerful means, of intimacy. The means matter. Ultimately the means are all that matter. Yes, we want to offer you opportunity, and it is critical to do it with intimacy.

Perhaps the most important reason we are communicating is the most personal reason: To communicate with Peny. Each day we speak together.

The content of our talks together varies broadly. Some evenings we review future workshops and seminars. We will often try out new techniques and meditations to make sure we are not "going too fast." Though we are never impatient, we are always enthusiastic — always eager.

Other times we work with Peny and her process and her programmings, though those times are less and less necessary. We spend time exploring philosophy and esoteric topics long into the night. Our energy combines with hers and we spiral beyond time and space on telepathic-like journeys. Then there are the times we laugh together and just have fun. Our relationship is truly one of loving friendship.

With the always changing form and context, our conversations may last hours or minutes. Most often the Channel's body is there in the gently darkened room, but, with all the travel, sometimes it's propped up on a hotel bed many miles away. Wherever his body is, our energy is always sitting quietly with Peny during our daily discussions.

What never changes is the intimacy Peny and we feel and actively create together. Friendship based on information and opportunity can be helpful — even valuable — but it will only last as long as the information and the opportunity is there. Such friendships, though wonderful, are linear.

The depth of friendship — the richness of friendship — the timelessness of friendship — the love of friendship — comes when the information and opportunity are blended with the magic of intimacy.

In our relationship with Peny, it is vital that we are close and tender and that we each actively create that closeness and tenderness. We softly speak of our love. Often.

Vulnerability and trust are integral parts of each of our interchanges together. Even at the height of the metaphysical circus and side show, our daily interactions became anchors of sensibilities: They reduced Peny's and the Channel's fear of humiliation.

Whether the conversation is profound or jocular, it is essential that the loving and caring be more than spoken. It is essential that it be demonstrated. Words can do more than just speak. Words can touch. Words can act. What gives them this life? The very love and care being expressed, if it's real. If it's real.

Intimacy is ultimately based on understanding. It is based on a desire to understand each other and a willingness to be understood.

For us, the *opportunity* of our relationship with Peny is the intimacy that we create with her. The *beauty* and the *wonder* of our relationship is the intimacy that she creates with us.

To you, Peny, *Lazaris Interviews* is like a remembrance of so many personal talks we have had together. Factually, the content and the context came from public interviews. Emotionally the meaning comes from many of our intimate talks with you.

To all of you, in *Lazaris Interviews* we answer a lot of different questions. The answers are intended to give you our point of view — to provide you with some information — to stimulate understanding and perception. More than the individual pieces of information and the opportunity they can encourage, the answers are intended to help you remember what you already know. The variety and brevity is intended to help you look beyond the information and to generate the intimacy that is there for you — that is waiting for you.

To each of you, we want to provide more than the *opportunity* to grow: We want to offer the *intimacy* of growing.

Peny, we thank you for the wonder and beauty of your love. We love you.

With Love and Peace ...

Lazaris

From Peny * ...

As we readied the interview books for printing, Lazaris asked me, as a favor to him, to share a piece of writing I did several years ago. I am usually reluctant to talk about my metaphysical experiences — it somehow seems trite these days to mention seeing ghosts, using telepathy, having out-of-body experiences, communicating with "dead" people — even the profound experiences with one's Higher Self are somehow becoming almost commonplace. I don't know quite what I think of all this yet.

At any rate, some close friends asked me to write a few lines about my spiritual odyssey, and I wrote this piece, in the third person. This piece primarily covers the time before Lazaris began channeling through Jach, which was October 3rd, 1974.

There had been a time when everything seemed like a brilliant confusion. Learning had always happened easily, and winning had always come almost as easily. Once a favorite teacher told her, "I feel sorry for you. Between your good luck and your high IQ, you'll never know the satisfaction of accomplishment over a difficult challenge."

---

* *Many of you have known Peny and Michaell as Peny and Michaell Prestini. For esoteric reasons they have changed their last name and now are Peny and Michaell North.*

At this time the purpose of life seemed to be learning the rules and then realizing that you were expected to know when and how to modify the rules without getting caught. They had told her that the point of life was to be virtuous, **good**, and polite, and pray to Jesus ... and always to be the top of her class.

They hadn't realized that too often the intelligence it takes to always be the top will expose the stupidity of the moral philosophy they simultaneously hope to instill. And then the confusion escalates.

The confusion is long past now, and only rarely does a piece of it drift to shore again like a torn plank from a long-sunk galleon. Sometimes when she tried to explain how she got from there to here, the paradoxes and octave shifts and reality blends would get so entangled she'd want to just throw up her hands and laugh. How could she tell them that the way to get to the far shore might have to involve letting your initial vessel sink and then having to trust the sea goddess herself to transport you back to solid shifting sands?

The focus of her world now was love, and she fully realized the saccharine threat of trying to talk about it. She knew it was difficult for people to understand the love between herself and Michaell and Jach, but it was so alive and real and even flexible that they themselves regarded it as a conscious friend. And, shifting another few octaves, was the dyad love she shared with Michaell, a state of being that still made her catch her breath as she watched it grow and stretch like a sentient molecule realizing it can evolve into a star.

Everything in her life centered around this warm pyramid of love and the pyramid itself, like a candle-lit Bedouin tent in the black night desert, gave her courage and energy to meet the Universe and its Dance of Chaos head-on. She didn't care anymore about being the top or winning or even what others thought of her. She **did** care about the love, and, as for the rest of it, she found it difficult to explain.

How could she tell them that it really **is** only all illusion on this planet? And, worse yet, how could she tell them that the trick of handling the illusion is to concentrate on one piece at a time and change it before your very eyes, and **then** realize you can't pat yourself on the back because you only magically transformed an illusion! The problem didn't keep her worrying, though, because she had long since realized she didn't owe them anything, and she knew she'd only dance the dance as long as it was fun.

She remembered the strange period when she'd realized, past the point of refutation, that reality was an illusion done with holograms and mirrors. The freedom of the realization had quickly darkened with a sense of meaninglessness that crept across her playground like the lengthening shadow of twilight. For awhile it looked like the night would win; for awhile it looked like her entry into Chapel Perilous had finally over-extended her wherewithal.

She was well aware of her dilemma. She had finally gone too far. She had broken all the rules of censorship and restriction "for your own good" and, like an errant child catching daddy dress up as Santa Claus, she had stumbled onto the emptiest and freest of understandings — there's no one out there to rescue me.

The abyss offers no tour guides. You do your own research. So, she studied what she could find on the few who had stood there, and confusion almost ended the search. It was Blavatsky, of all the loving spirits, who finally forced her to see that there were only, after all, **two** options.

The cosmos supports simplicity without exception.

The options are layered in paradoxes so thick and convoluted that they end up looking identical at the surface. At the surface they both say "surrender." But underneath one lies sheer insanity — the insanity of giving away your power in order to have someone else do it all for you, the insanity of apathy and meaninglessness and eternal boredom and fear. That option has the prettiest facade, though, because it beckons you with pictures of idyllic childhood, and it is exceedingly tempting.

She had picked up this pretty little picture and considered signing up. She had stood there holding this tempting option like a beautiful music box begging to be listened to, and she had leaned out into the icy winds of conclusive evidence at the abyss and felt the pull of the yawning void, the space and shape of consciousness that is epitomized on the physical plane by the astronomical black holes of space. And just at the critical moment, when the first few notes of the **mechanical** music box reached her ears, she began to hum her own song instead ... and the lights switched on.

Sometime, if you care to ask, I'll tell you how she created a complex and very, very magical world full of present-tense activity. A world of art and books and music. A world of communicating with "dead" entities like Anäis Nin and Colette, a world of playing with long-forgotten goddesses like Isis and the Crone, a world of swirling creativity that clearly recognizes self-pity and boredom as the enemies and cheerfully reckons with them.

The "how" of it all is not as important as the "why," and she was extremely wary of anyone who told her not to ask "why." First you create the type of space you want to play in, and **then** you manifest the toys. Lazaris had told her that so many years ago, and she laughed with delight as she saw the space taking shape.

Sometimes, very late at night when she was having a session with Lazaris, she felt the love between them like sheer voltage, and she thanked herself again for setting that

beautiful music box back down again at the edge of the abyss
so long ago.

I love you.

Peny
Los Angeles, 1988

Lazaris Explains Lazaris

What We Are Not — What We Are — How We Communicate
Why We Communicate (Peny) — Why Else We Communicate
Our Purpose

Many years ago Lazaris recorded a beautiful cassette tape explaining who he is and why he is here. With so much speculation offered and so many conclusions reached about what channeling is really all about, it is perhaps appropriate that Lazaris explain Lazaris and that we each draw our own conclusions.

A s we say, we officially began communicating through Jach, the one we call the Channel, on October 3rd, 1974. We had made contact with him much earlier in that year through his own meditative approaches — and indeed much to his surprise! Our initial message to him (as he quite accurately reports it) was: "We will call you ... not for you to call us." Through that period of time we rather made the initial adjustments — and completed the final adjustments — such as to make possible our communication without creating any distress or harm to the physical, mental or psychological form of the one who is the Channel.

Prior to that timing (according to your particular schedules it would be during several of his previous lifetimes) we had made contact with the Channel to nudge, to gently nudge and suggest (much without his knowing) certain evolutionary developments in preparation for this timing of October, 1974. During his current lifetime, in his childhood and early adolescence, again we were ever so gently, ever so subtly nudging. For above all we did not want to create any distress. We wanted only to create the opportunity for his growth, for our interaction, and for the growth and evolution for those with whom we would be speaking.

We are the only one, as we have suggested, from our levels of awareness who has ever or who will ever communicate with your planet, and the only one we shall ever come through is the Channel. We have taken "time," and a precious great deal of it according to your standards, to make that communication most beneficial, most elegant, most clear. Therefore, we are satisfied and need not explore and expand to channel through any other form in any other capacity.

What We Are Not

First of all, we are not physical, nor have we ever been, though many have asked us where our lifetimes were, or when we were on the planet, suggesting we must have been in Atlantis or perhaps Lemuria before. But the answer, always the same is: "No, we have not been physical." We have not been on your Physical Plane at any time of its history — nor, for that matter, on any other planet or system that supports physical life.

Now we rather stress that point, though perhaps it would be very simple for us just to say, "Oh, we existed on some extra terrestrial planet," or, "We existed in some time past (that would never be traceable)." That would satisfy many, but it would not be the truth. Physical beings have great difficulty dealing with the idea that there are consciousnesses — and intelligent consciousnesses at that — that have opted not to develop in any way that resembles a physical development.

Now for those of you who live in the United States, we pose the question, "Is it conceivable to you that there are people who live from birth to death and never, ever set foot upon the United States?" Answer: "Of course. Naturally so. There are millions of them." Then when asked, "Is it possible that there are those consciousnesses who exist in their reality who have never been physical?" why is it so inconceivable? Why does that seem so ponderously strange? We would suggest that just as there are those who have not been in the United States, there are those who have not been physical ... and we are one of them.

You see, in the development of consciousness, you, as a spark of consciousness, make certain decisions. Among the earlier decisions that you make is: In the process of your growth, do you want to do it in a bodied form, a physicality, or not? Obviously, those of you listening to this tape, for the majority, have decided you do, and thus you have, and thus you are physical. However, we broached that question, and we decided no, and therefore we are not, nor ever have been, physical.

What else are we not? Well, we are not a guru, and we are not a master. Oh, dear no! We rather moved beyond those levels long ago, as you would call it in time, in our awareness of our growth. Therefore, we are not intending ever to be followed, to develop disciples, to be anyone's guru, master or leader.

It was expressed once very nicely by a particular person with whom we have talked. Speaking with someone who had not yet heard or known much about us, the person was asked, "Ah, you're a follower of Lazaris?" After a poignant pause, the individual responded, "No, I'm not a follower. I am a friend." And that's what we much prefer.

There's nothing wrong with gurus or masters — nor do we object to their existence. We suggest, however, that eventually each individual, each consciousness, must come to the conclusion that indeed it is its own guru, its own master. Therefore, out of respect for you, we refuse to fulfill that role even for a moment. Out of respect for ourselves, we refuse to go back to that level, but rather insist upon soaring forth in our own growth.

We are also not a father figure, though many would like to make us such to replace the absence of the father who wasn't there, or the inadequacies of the one who was there. But again, we steadfastly and with great patience resist this role. You see, if you attempt to put us into that position, then you will have to treat us as a father, and eventually reject, and eventually create the problems of self-respect. Once again, out of respect for you and your consciousness, we smile, we nod, and say, "No, thank you. Please, we would much rather be your friend — not your father."

What We Are

"We are a spark of consciousness" is perhaps the best way to describe us. Content without form. We are a spark of consciousness that exists and is aware of its existence, that creates thought, that creates reality, just as you are consciousness that creates thought and creates reality. We do it with a greater level of awareness, and we do it without form. That is the difference.

Also, one could well say that we are multi-leveled consciousness, and thus refer to ourselves as "we" — not because we're imperial, but simply because we are aware of the multi-levels of our existence. When you make reference to yourself, you often use the word "I", because at any one moment of consciousness you are most often aware of yourself in the singularity of your physical existence, though intellectually you know you exist on the Astral, and on the higher levels of consciousness, by whatever names you give them. But at any moment — from one to the next — you experience those moments linearly.

In our consciousness, we experience them exponentially. Therefore, for us to say "I" seems rather meaningless, for we are aware of our existence on multiple levels, multiple levels of awareness — and out of deference to and respect for ourselves, we refer to the multiplicities as "we". Indeed, we have suggested upon occasion that if we were ever to be physical, we most certainly would have to be a number of people for we could not all fit into one body form.

Does that mean we're a very large spark of consciousness? A spark is a spark. It is neither large nor small. It has no form. We are simply content. We suggest that you are also a spark of consciousness. You also exist not only on the Physical, Astral, Causal and Mental Planes — your expanded playground of awareness — but you exist on all the other levels of awareness as well. You exist on the same levels of awareness on which we exist. The difference: We know it. You don't ... yet.

Well, in the Human Potential Movement and in many other systems of growth — whether they are actually dealing with the potential of the human or not — there is often this attempt to categorize. "My guru is more important than yours. My master is at a higher level than yours." Many get into this hierarchical structure of what's what and who's who and who's above whom, etc. In one regard, which is more evolved, the bulb of the tulip, the stem, the leaves, or the flower itself? Indeed, it becomes ludicrous to try to say the bulb is more or less evolved than the tulip petal that eventually unfolds.

Also, we have found that those people to whom it is important to know if it is level #10 or #25 or #36 probably could never understand the meaning and the significance therein, even if we did tell them. What we suggest is this: We define from our perspective — and you can do so as you like — that there is a Physical Reality, and then an Astral Reality, and beyond that what we have described as the Causal Plane of Reality where "cause and effect" is initiated and expanded. Then there is the Mental Plane of Reality, upon which are placed most of what are called "heavens" (either Christian, Buddhist, Eastern-religioned or Middle Eastern-religioned heavens, paradises, *nirvanas*, utopias), and the major gods of the major religions of your reality.

These four planes we call the Lower Worlds — not because they're "less than," but as a point of distinction between them and the Higher Worlds. This distinction also is a distinction of who creates them. We suggest that all of you who are physical, and all of you who have been physical, are responsible for the creative energies that have brought about the Physical, Astral, Causal and Mental Planes of Reality. Beyond that exist the Higher Realms, to which some attach names (usually Eastern, tongue-tying names that are difficult to pronounce), planes which would be labeled effectively as the Fifth, Sixth, Seventh, Eighth, and Ninth Planes of Reality.

The numbers increase ... forever. For indeed there is no ceiling. There is no limit to the development of consciousness, and similarly no limit to the development of the Planes of Reality. Thus, often to the question *What Plane are you on?* we suggest: "Pick a number. We'll be there."

Let us just say this: We exist on a plane of reality that is far beyond that which we call the Lower Worlds, far beyond that which would be labeled by any system as the "Soul Planes" of Reality.

Perhaps that would be sufficient, for our goal is not to impress you with the number or numbers of planes of our realities, but to assist you by providing insight, insight that we beseech you to accept not because "Lazaris said so" or "a friend of mine got a lot of help," but rather because what we suggest works for you. As it works for you and allows you to explore your life more fully and more completely, then the matter of "which Plane" diminishes and your ability to create success, your ability to be the whole and total being that you are, similarly increases.

We often look at ourselves (figuratively, for we do not have eyes) as energy that creates thought. We do not think. And those of you who have spoken with us for lengthy periods of time, and those for only recent times, notice that you never hear us say, "Well, we think this," or "Let us think about that." You see, we don't think. Thinking involves time. Thinking involves "now" and "then." Therefore, we create thought, and we transmit that created thought in the hopes that it might perhaps be of assistance in our communications with you.

How We Communicate

Well, how do we communicate? That is also of curiosity to many. We would first suggest that we never enter the body of the Channel, for that's not necessary. When you turn on your television set and watch the evening news, you don't for a moment suspect that the anchor person is sitting inside that little box. You know full well that he/she is sitting in a station somewhere and is talking to a camera, which is recording and then sending those signals through the air to your local receiving station — which then transmits the signal to your television set — sometimes even by videotape (how fascinating!) or film.

We would liken our communication to that process. We do not enter the physical form of the Channel. We don't get anywhere near that Physical Plane of reality, but rather, we connect energies that are thoughts into a system of vibration that we then transmit through the cosmos and the various levels. The system of vibration then enters your reality through the Mental Plane, then drifts down, in its way, to the Physical Plane — much as a television signal to the antenna — and then is amplified and comes out of the vocal chords, the mouth, and the speaking structure of that which is the Channel.

In its amplification and sequencing it sounds suspiciously like words. Your ears pick it up and you hear words. Do we speak? No, we transmit blips and bleeps of energy, if you will, that through their amplification sound like words — and through those blips and bleeps and transmissions of energies, that sound like words, you absorb ideas, and thus we communicate.

Why We Communicate ... Peny

Well, why do we communicate? Well, the first reason, and to us the most special reason, is in order to talk to the one who is known as Peny. Now initially that might sound a bit trite. "Well, if you came to talk with one person, why are you bothering talking to the rest of us, and why are you bothering making this tape at all?"

So let us explain that a bit more fully. As we said at the beginning of this recording, we began nudging the Channel several of his lifetimes ago, and more specifically and more directly in his current life. We began an initial contact with him meditatively in early 1974, and then finally had our "coming out party," so to speak, on October 3rd. All of this, in your sequence of events, took many hundreds of years. In our sequence without time, well, one can't even say it took a moment. All of this we did so that we might talk with the one Peny.

Early on in our communication she asked us, "What is it that I can do or that we (meaning herself and the Channel) can do to assist you in accomplishing that which you are here to accomplish? What should we do to get out of the way so that you might do for the planet that which you came to do?"

We smiled and chuckled a bit and proceeded to explain that we had come primarily to talk with her. We had no mission to save anything or anyone, but rather we came to talk and chat with her. We said that if, for the remainder of her physical existence, we only spoke with her and indeed no one ever heard of our existence or talked with us, our mission would have been accomplished — but that if she would like us to talk with others, we'd be more than happy to do so.

She did, we are, and you're hearing this recording. That is because Peny is a very special being to us, a being whom we have been aware of for many, many of her lifetimes — though not interfering or involving ourselves — a being who has developed her own evolutionary path, and who has proceeded along that path very joyously and very successfully.

She is a very special person, one who touches us very deeply — the one we came to touch because of her particular focus in this lifetime, a focus which she attempted many lifetimes ago and did not succeed in accomplishing, a focus which she tenaciously decided to do again. Therefore, she has returned three additional times beyond that which was necessary in order to accomplish this focus. Thus we wanted to talk with her, to be with her, to share her experience and our experience, as in this lifetime that focus shall be accomplished — completing a task begun thousands of years ago in her reality.

Many of you are aware of the very special energy of love, of caring, and of insight that Peny provides. That love, that caring, that insight, that gem of an energy that is Peny: It is to experience and to bask in that, that we have primarily come to communicate.

Why Else We Communicate

Since we have never been physical and have a very natural curiosity, we rather also wanted to learn about your physical reality, but did not want to have to do that through the limitations of form, a decision, by the by, with which we are ever increasingly pleased. It is not that we don't appreciate and respect that which you go through as physical beings, but exactly because we do respect and appreciate it that we are quite proud of our decision ever so "long" ago not to go through that hustle you call physicality.

But since we did want to learn, and therefore chose to do it in this manner, we decided to make that also a two-way experience, such that we not only are learning about your Physical Plane, but also are giving you an opportunity to see your own reality from our perspective. Therefore, there is an exchange: For what you give us in awareness of your reality, we are more than happily exchanging our perspective in offering you insight into ours.

That is why we do workshops and seminars. We want very much to have the opportunity to share with you, as specifically as we can, our observations of your reality, as you have created it, offering you perhaps insights and suggestions as to how you might alter your perspective, change your approach, such as to create a reality more to your own liking.

Those of you who have been with us notice that we never tell you what to do. We only make suggestions. We suggest this, and we suggest that, for there is no judgment that you must accomplish anything. We respect you to know what is best for you, and, therefore, if you want to create the reality you're creating, we are not going to tell you otherwise, but we will suggest perhaps more helpful or beneficial ways of approaching your reality.

No issue is too large or too small. No human question is too intelligent or too dumb. For, indeed, the curiosity we have about the Physical Plane and the human form does not result in boredom, for boredom requires time. Nor do we get impatient. Similarly, impatience requires time.

We also enjoy talking with people about their past lives. We hesitate as we say the term, for it is a misnomer since all lifetimes are concurrent. All lifetimes are simultaneous and are only labeled "past" for the convenience of categorizing them. We enjoy sharing that perspective, because, you see, without time we can be aware of your past, present and future, and therefore we can dip in and tap in for you, and explore with you that which is there to be discovered.

Our intent in talking of lifetimes is not to entertain, though indeed many of the lifetimes are extremely entertaining. Rather, the purpose is to provide you with a grasp and an understanding, and a perspective of fitting them together in a larger scope, such that you might benefit and grow, not only from knowing what the lifetimes have been, but also from learning how to work with them. This is an integral part of a life reading. Such a consultation shows you how you might augment those very positive and powerful aspects of what you've been in other experiences, and also assists you in learning how to diminish those less positive influences.

Many who talk of lifetimes want to suggest that they control you. Quite to the contrary, you control yourself, but past lifetimes augment or they influence your perceptions and perspectives. As you can become aware of the tint of your rose-colored glasses, so you can compensate and adjust for that to allow yourself a clearer vision.

With many with whom we talk we share their blockages, those things that get in the way of creating that absolutely delightfully successful life. You see, in order to overcome hurdles, first you have to construct them. But then you forget that you were the one who constructed them, and you keep stumbling over them in the dark. So, if we can perhaps help shed light and point out those particular hurdles, and help you understand why you created them, then you can learn and allow yourself to glide over them with grace, and then in time satisfy yourself that you have learned how to overcome them ... and then get rid of them altogether.

Our emphasis in talking with people is on providing techniques. We never tell people: "This is the way it is, and therefore accept it," but rather we explain: "This is the way you created it, and therefore, if you want it, accept it. If you don't like what you've created, here's about 15 or 20 different ways in which you can work with it" — because the truth is that you create everything, and, therefore, you have the reins in your hands.

There are so many aspects, so many messages you give yourself, and many times you overlook them. An example is the importance of dreams. Dreams are the coded messages that your subconscious and Higher Conscious attempt to give you. You see, until you consciously grow, in many ways your negative ego has been Chairman of the Board, so to speak, for all of your life. It is fairly comfortable in its cushy chair. When you come along and decide, "All right, now I'm ready to grow, ready to expand and to explore my own spiritual development," you, in a sense, are kicking the negative ego out as Chairman of the Board and replacing it with your conscious self, which is — how do you say? — fueled by the subconcious, the unconscious, and the Higher Conscious selves or minds. The negative ego is often "a bit resentful" and "jealous" of being dethroned and will do what it can to throw up interference.

This is what is happening with the person who, in their meditation, gets very clearly that they are God, or God's specific messenger to save the planet. That is where the negative ego gets involved in meditations and altered states, kicking up very negative and very destructive information. This ego gets in the way, and therefore the Higher Consciousness and subconscious mind, being shrewder, figure out ways of sending you coded messages, ways of alerting you to things to pay attention to, alerting you to things to watch out for and to be aware of. These coded messages often come through dreams.

These coded messages also respond in the health and physical well-being of the body. To stub your toe is many times a message: Watch your footing. To develop a problem with your eyes is often telling you you're afraid of seeing something. Ringing in your ears could be a statement that you're not willing to listen, or that you ought to pay attention more to what you're hearing.

And then it could mean any number of other things instead. To insist that you know and insist that you figure it all out by yourself is perhaps asking a bit too much. So it is that we enjoy exchanging our perspective to rather help you understand ways and means of decoding these messages that are so frequently given.

Similarly: Meditations. They are a beautiful technique of growth. For those of you who want to develop, we are more than happy to assist you in unraveling both the amount of dogma and the amount of information that have been disseminated through aeons of time. We provide many of you with little personal and unique approaches that can help *you*, but not necessarily everyone, with your meditative approaches.

Basically, in our exchange of perspective, we want to offer you an opportunity to see yourself more clearly and an opportunity to do as you wish — an opportunity to realize not only that you hold the reins of your reality, but also that you can actually creatively do something about it.

Also, we like to talk with people about their focuses. We use that term "focus" because words like "purpose," "task," "mission," or "duty" sound so very ominous, as though someone up there opened a fortune cookie and rather gave you an assignment: "This is your job. Don't come back 'til it's done!" The word "focus" implies much more completely the self-choice that is involved.

Like the focus of a lens, you can wide-angle or zoom. You can slip filters of varying sizes and shapes and colors in front of the lens to change the perspective. Indeed, you also have the opportunity to refocus on something else entirely. And though it is true that each lifetime has a focus — indeed seven of them — you have the choices and you have the options.

That brings us to the final reason we are communicating, and that is to offer alternatives, to offer choices. You see, you do create your own reality, and many of you know that, and many of you feel that and experience that, but often you have not considered the choices that are available.

Often you are being told that you must make this happen, or that you must do that, or that you are supposed to use your creativity, your power, and your spirituality this way or that. That's all well and good, and the intentions of those that tell you what to do may well be very clear, but we would suggest that you deserve to know your options, to know the choices, to know that which is available to you. You deserve to have the choice as to whether you want to *make* your reality work, or — as we would suggest — *let* it work metaphysically. You deserve the choice as to the means — as to the means of letting yourself have success, of letting yourself have joy, and of letting yourself have a personal alternative spirituality.

Our Purpose

What is our purpose, our focus, as we would call it? It is not to save the planet. The planet, indeed, can take good care of itself. It has been doing so and will continue to do so. The Earth was taking care of itself long before each of you hearing this was born into this lifetime, and it will be doing so long after you die from this one. We are not here to save you, either. You can do that. At this point, let us say this: We are simply here because it's fun — because we enjoy it, and because of the "Aha!" moments of realization and pleasure.

You see, about 1% of our energy (if one were to be dividing it into percentages at all) is involved in communicating with the physical world, your Earth plane, your planet, your planet only. The remainder of our energies are involved in doing exactly the same thing — communicating, sharing, offering choices of alternatives, and offering perspectives — with those consciousnesses who have long since moved beyond your physical plane and who are on the evolutionary patterns of the higher levels.

So our purpose, our focus, is to have fun, to enjoy the "Aha!" of your realization, and to bask in that energy of your growth. No judgments. No demands. Our purpose is simply to have fun, and indeed if it were not fun, we would not do so. And it is not your responsibility to make it fun for us — for yourself, yes — but for us, no. For above all, we do indeed take full and total responsibility for that which we experience.

We have fun. We do not want to save anything. Perhaps the only thing we'd want to save is your right to make choices, and your right to decide what is best for you. Perhaps we'd want to save your right to take full and total responsibility for your reality, and indeed that is perhaps what we're about.

When it comes right down to it, we want to be your friend, and as a friend to enjoy your experiences as you enjoy them, to laugh with your joy, to be there to help you when you cry. We want to be able to give insight, understanding, awareness, and to receive the joy of your experience of yourself. To lead you? No. To master you? No. To have you praise and honor us? *Definitely not.* To be a friend.

To be a friend.

With love and peace ...

Lazaris

Channeling &
The New Spirituality

Channeling: Why Now?

Q: There is a tremendous increase in the popularity of channeling. Why do you think this is? Does it fit into a larger pattern?

Lazaris: It does fit into a larger pattern, absolutely so. This is a New Age or a New Spirituality. There is a newness that is continuously coming.

The seat of power, the point of consciousness, is located in the conscious mind. More and more your reality is a product of your conscious thoughts and feelings.

This is more than theory or an interesting philosophy. Mystics have been foretelling of a time of conscious power since awareness began. Physicists have been proving the power of conscious thought and feeling for over half a century.

The larger pattern is that you are moving into a New Age — a New Spirituality — where you consciously create your own reality. This truth is becoming more and more real. In reaction and response to this realness, people are asking for help — spiritual help. They are discovering and calling out to their Higher Selves. They are reaching beyond their Higher Selves as they ask for help. They are creating that help in the form of channeling.

Channeling runs the range, just like every other activity in life. There are the good ones and the not-so-good ones.

On the down side, there are those who see this as a tremendous moneymaking opportunity. Others have looked at it as a tremendous power trip, and therefore have hopped on the bandwagon quite erroneously, quite fraudulently. Others are sincere in intention, but are not having the connection they ought to have or the clarity they ought to have, and therefore are channeling inadequately or inappropriately. There are also those who are allowing very high energies, very powerful energies to travel through and to put the information forth.

This also is a part of the pattern, for, you see, it is important that you as individuals learn discernment. You are barraged with all kinds of channeled information, and, in that sense, you have to pick and choose. Which works? Which doesn't? Which is valid? Which is not? Which can help? Which does not? Therefore, you are still responsible. Therefore, you are still powerful.

If every shred of channeled information from every channeled source were accurate and correct, and therefore you could "just accept it because it is so," there would be no responsibility left for the human being. That would be terribly unfair. So therefore, the opportunity of discernment, the opportunity of choice, the opportunity of finding the answers is part of what this New Age is.

Secondly, it is part of the New Spirituality. More and more people in your world, particularly in the United States, have fulfilled their basic needs. When you were children you were told, "If you just get the right job and the right education and the right marriage, then the world will be 'golden.'" You listened to what you were told, and you did what you were told. It still wasn't enough.

You turned to your traditional sources of spirituality, which hitherto had been the Judeo-Christian ethic. It was an answer, but not enough of an answer. You didn't abandon it necessarily. You stretched beyond it.

We suggest that the New Spirituality is that search, is that seeking of God/Goddess/All That Is, a force that is more than limited religious concepts. You are searching for and seeking a grander sense of wholeness, a grander sense of channeling, a grander activity where forces from other levels offer their input and information. So yes, channeling is increasing.

*Alan Vaughan, **Whole Life Monthly**, Santa Monica, California*

Q: Why do you think there's so much channeling going on now?

Lazaris: There are several reasons. Perhaps the most important is the Age that you are in and the eagerness of people to grow, the eagerness of you as human beings — whether you consider yourself to be metaphysical or not — to reach, to stretch, to search, to try to discover that "something more."

We would also suggest that within humanity as a whole, worldwide, there is an upsurgence of energy in the seeking of answers, but also in the seeking of a sense of God, what we refer to as God/Goddess/All That Is. There is a desire to have a more intimate, more meaningful, more powerful relationship with God/Goddess/All That is.

That energy is nationally very powerful, but also internationally it is increasingly powerful. In a sense it is like a magnet that is calling, putting out a vibration that is attracting more and more "spiritual help" (not spiritual doingness, but spiritual help) to assist you in completing the task that you've laid forth for yourselves, to help you understand what's going on.

The second reason is because it has been invited. Why all of this is happening is because you as human consciousnesses have invited it, have opened your minds,

have opened your hearts, have opened your consciousnesses to a willingness to grow and a willingness to
stretch in this way. You have opened to this kind of
help, this kind of input, this kind of information. That's
the second reason.

*Brian Enright/Lisa Michelle Guest, **Los Angeles** &*
***Orange County Resources**, Los Angeles*

Channeling & Discernment

azaris: There is a series of questions to ask and to
answer for yourself. First: "Are the teachings consistently unlimited? Or are the teachings limited in
that they give you the sense that you are less than you
are?" There are those who will tell you only of your
limitations, making you feel totally inadequate and "less
than." There are those who will attempt to convince
you that you are totally unevolved, helpless, and hopeless. Similarly, they will tell you they are the one sent to
save you, or that they are the only one who can really
help. Be wary.

Secondly, you want to take what they tell you and
ask, "Can I apply this? Can I use this? Or is this useless
mind-babble?" To sit around and talk about ancient
civilizations and tell you about what they did in Atlantis and Lemuria is curious and interesting, but you need
to ask: "What's it going to do for me? How is it going to
help me become more of who I am?"

Q: For
people who
are just begin-
ning to inves-
tigate trance
channels,
what kind of
guidelines
would you
give?

Thirdly ask, "As I apply what's being said, am I happier? Is my life working better?"

Fourthly, ask yourself, "When I come away from the experience, am I feeling and am I thinking more hopefully?" A lot of people follow their heart: "What's in my heart?" Your heart doesn't always tell you the truth. Your heart will tell you your feelings, but you need to think, also. You need to think. "Based on what I think *and* what I feel, how has this experience uplifted me? Has the experience made me more of who I am, or has it made me less?"

A lot of metaphysics teaches you, "Don't think. Just feel. Just experience. Shut down your mind." Don't shut it down! Think, think, think, read and regard. In fact, stop for a moment and try to feel without thinking. If you are honest with yourself, you cannot do it because it cannot be done. In order to feel, you must think. You must conjure images, audibles, or kinesthetics — you must think. Similarly, you cannot think without also feeling. The two processes are linked. In theory, it might sound nice to "just feel, just listen to your heart," but in function it is not only impossible, it is inadvisable. Let yourself feel and think. Be conscious of both.

Three additional questions to consider: "Is the message consistent? Is the personality of the entity or energy consistent? Are the teachings without contradiction?" Because there is no time, a channeled source that is viable will not be "in a bad mood today." Also, their teachings may build and expand. They may not teach everything they know at one time, but the teaching will not be inconsistent and should not contradict itself.

If you will honestly evaluate these seven questions, you will have a valuable set of guidelines to follow.

*Craig Lee, **LA Weekly**, Los Angeles*

Lazaris: Well, is there a danger here that people can give away their power? Yes. There is a grand danger of that. One of the very sad things that is happening in this field (which we suggest is only part of the process) is that not only are there those who are turning over their power, but also there are those who are wanting to take it.

Q: Isn't there a danger that people will have a tendency to listen to a channel's reality and become dependent on that rather than seeking out their own truth? And if so, what can you recommend to them to stay clear?

There are certain consciousnesses that are either in the realm of being quite fraudulent, or who feel they are perhaps legitimate, but are coming, in fact, from a very low level — a trickster reality — who are basically out there to rob power, to take power from people.

This is a danger in the field of metaphysics, but it is a danger in any field. In school, you can give your power away to any number of teachers. At work, you can give your power to any number of supervisors or bosses. It is a danger, but not such a danger that you should turn away from metaphysics, spirituality, or growth any more than you would consider stopping your education or never working again. You might change and learn from different teachers, you might find a new job, but you would not stop learning or working due to this danger. Eventually people who give away their power come to their senses and stop doing it.

The thing to do is to discern. Listen to the message. Listen to the consistency of the message. Listen to the consistency of the personality. Are you being told to limit yourself? Is the information or motivation based upon fear? Ask yourself not just these questions, but these *kinds* of questions.

Also, figure out: Are you being asked to have faith? Are you being told, "Have faith in us. If you just have faith in us, then we'll make your life work … "? Are you being told that they'll "do it for you"? Is the channeled consciousness saying, "Look, I will see to it that your life works." Or, "I will make your life work. I will do it for you. You just have faith in me. I'll take care of everything."

If you're given those kinds of messages, be leery. Be very leery. You see, we talk to people, and we say, "We won't do it for you. We'll help you do it, but we will not do it for you." If a channeled energy says they will do it for you, or will see to it that it's done for you, at that point we'd put on the brakes fast and furiously. Most definitely, we would.

Brian Enright/Lisa Michelle Guest, Los Angeles & Orange County Resources, Los Angeles

Q: How can one tell the difference between negativity and normal skepticism — or is skepticism stated pessimism?

Lazaris: Skepticism is not necessarily stated pessimism at all. Skepticism is wonderful. It has a most marvelous quality.

Do you realize how wonderful the skeptics are in your reality — all those people who think your Doom and Gloom ideas are a bunch of craziness? Do you realize how many times California would have fallen off into the ocean if all those who believe in such things prevailed? Thank God for the skeptics who thought that was a bunch of silliness!

Skepticism is healthy, particularly in the carnival atmosphere that you have in your metaphysics. Part of the reason the carnival has been able to exist is that people misunderstood the dictum: "Do not judge."

You have thought that non-judgment means you shouldn't have opinions, you shouldn't be discerning, and you shouldn't even make any statement. After all, how do you know that the entity channeling through isn't the reincarnation of Tutankhamen's cat? How can you absolutely be sure, eh? ... {laughter} ...

Because you've got a mind — that's how you can be sure! ... {laughter} ... It's amazing to us. There are people out there claiming to channel the 12th level of the 14th vision of the 13th dimension of Venus, for crying out loud. Oh, come now! A bunch of fish are channeling through someone else! Well, how do you know they haven't? Because you're able to think! Because you've got some sensibility about you. Each of you, even if you don't have a full sense of understanding about metaphysics, has a beautiful, healthy skepticism.

What's the difference between negative ego and skepticism? Negative ego is out to destroy you. Skepticism is a part of you that's saying, "Maybe it doesn't make sense because it's nonsense."

And we suggest, "Be skeptical." With us, we would tell you, "Don't take what we say because Lazaris says it. Take it because it works. Take it because it makes sense."

What's important is for you to learn what works. Sometimes these things that are so far out that they don't make any sense are just that: non-sense. You never thought of it. It doesn't make any sense. It doesn't make any logical sense because there isn't any kind of logic to it. Now admittedly a lot of metaphysics doesn't fit *linear* logic, but there is not a single truth in metaphysics that doesn't fit *exponential* logic.

Have skepticism. Don't just take what we say because we say it. Try it out. See if it works. Find out what does work for you. If what we say works for you, grand. Accept it on that basis. Use the same discernment with everything else. Apply the same standard we suggest for us to everything that you work with. Be skeptical — healthily skeptical.

The negative ego is out to destroy you. Skepticism is out to help you put things in perspective. Be healthily skeptical. Be open, be willing, but keep an ear cocked and a sharp eye.

Anonymous Question, **Seattle Evening with Lazaris,** *1987*

Q: Are there lower forms of entities and higher forms in the sense of lower and higher consciousnesses being channeled?

Lazaris: Most definitely. That's often a mistake of the eager seeker. Back in the '60s, there were hippies and the free love they advocated. Then and now, you laugh at them and look down on them. But those people were courageous. They were gutsy people who were willing so say "No!" to the system and the tradition. They dared to say, "There's another way to live. There's another way to be. There's another way to live ... and I don't know what it is, but at least I'm going to try to find out." And they went out, and they were ridiculed and laughed at, but they were beautiful people, willing to try to find that piece of spirituality.

Then there is the "me-ism" of the '70s which everybody looks at and says, "Oh, how could they be so crass?" But your desire to grow was so beautiful, so beautiful, so desperately authentic, that when anyone came along and said, "I've got an answer," you flocked to him or her.

People were so eager that they went down all kinds of dead-end alleys, but still they weren't fools or stupid. We feel a tremendous compassion for them. In their eagerness they got misled in their growth and were left standing there with egg on their faces. Even those who found some answers, but not enough, were still eager to grow.

In this channeling area, there's still that eagerness. If someone is channeling, people are so eager to grow that they assume it's all valid information. They don't want to believe that there are some channeled entities that are unevolved, if well-intentioned.

Some lower Astral entities are tricksters. They come through initially offering some marvelously wonderful insight, and you're hooked. Then they start screwing your life up, messing your life up, leading you into a total shambles. Some may be telling the truth as they see it, but it's from a limited scope. They — the entities — need to grow more as consciousnesses.

*Craig Lee, **LA Weekly**, Los Angeles*

The Personal Desire To Channel

Lazaris: There are some inherent activities here that one has to look at. We know that in the metaphysical community right now the concept of dealing with processing is becoming oh, ever so tiresome, yes? But it is a very necessary part of growth.

You see, in the '70s you got caught up in the "me-ism" of it, we understand. We don't criticize; we simply observe. In the '80s you moved beyond that.

Now, however, many of you don't want to process any more. You don't want to have to look at your feelings. You don't want to look at your emotions. Yes, you want all the "goodies," you want all the benefits, that

Q: In trying to learn to channel ourselves and to grow, is there any inherent danger in terms of unwelcome entities, and how do you handle that?

all that processing brought and might bring, yet you don't want to have to actually do it.

Therefore, the idea of people wanting to learn to channel can be both very exciting and very frightening. On one hand, the idea of your tapping into your own Higher Self or tapping into your counselors — your guides or guardian angels — is very exciting because you will once again begin to process. You will once again start working on understanding yourselves and the reality you are creating. Channeling information from deeper levels of your being will help you dig deeper into yourselves and your psyches.

On the other hand, it can be frightening if you channel for inappropriate reasons. You can really hurt yourself and your growth. You could really hurt others and their growth.

We know, above all, that you create your own reality. Many say that, therefore, you cannot hurt other people. Even though you do create it all, you create it so you can have impact on others. Those are the "rules" you created.

You do have impact. We shan't discuss that more fully here, but in another time and another space we will. It is frightening if you channel an inadequate or destructive energy — as you say, if you deal with unwelcome entities.

There are concerns, some very powerful concerns. Be aware of them.

First of all, you still do have a negative ego. People can get in touch with — woo! — a high, powerful entity that is nothing more than their own negative ego playing games! Those who sit down with a *ouija* board can *start* getting this "very powerful information." They begin to trust, and then they get nothing more than scuttlebutt, or worse: erroneous and harmful information. So interference can happen when one is beginning to channel.

The first thing to watch out for and to figure out is: "Where is my negative ego? What is my negative ego about? What are the games my negative ego usually plays?" It's not hard to figure out. The negative ego basically is dumb. It obviously is because it does the same thing over and over again.

Look at the problem that you have in your life right now. Really, what is the basic obstacle you have to your success? Whether it's in your job, or whether it's an obstacle to learning to channel, or whether it's in reaching a higher sense of your spirituality, what is the basic problem? What was your problem 10 years ago? It's the same thing, yes? It has different ingredients, but your negative ego does the same old stuff over and over again. It doesn't know any more than that.

So if you know what your negative ego is up to, then you can handle it so as to clear out its impact. You can process — dealing with the emotions, dealing with your thinking, looking at your beliefs and attitudes — figuring out what your ego is doing. You can process the child in you, the adolescent in you, and the parent in you (in Transactional Analysis terminology). You can learn about reality and clear out the mass consciousness and release it. You can clear the consensus reality out of the way and then release that negative ego so as to create a clearer flow of energy. That is point one.

Point two is to realize that you can get hooked up with delusions of grandeur. The trickster can indeed become involved. Therefore, one has to be clear in that way as well.

So what we suggest here is that you can hurt yourself by running into a wall, by listening to the delusions of grandeur, by listening to the negative ego, by thinking

> "Channeling runs the range just like every other activity in life. There are the good ones and the not-so-good ones ...

> "Some Lower Astral entities are tricksters. They come through initially offering some marvelously wonderful insight, and you're hooked. Then they start screwing up your life ... "

that you are channeling more than you are. There are certain things to be aware of and some technique to use.

Be aware, first of all, and listen to the information being communicated: Is it inconsistent? Is the message inconsistent or contradictory? Is it moody? Is it useless or harmful to you? Is it limiting to you? Is it making you feel hopeless or helpless? Is it making you feel unhappy about yourself and your future?

If it is any of those negations, then we would be very wary. If it is uplifting, if it is expanding, if it is allowing you to be more than you have been, then we would pay closer attention.

Secondly, does it work? Is the information of value? Is the psychic input that is coming to you actually panning out? Do the techniques, the approaches, or the suggestions offered actually work? Do the prognostications really come to pass? If they do pan out, listen. Otherwise, be wary.

Thirdly, assess whether the information expands or contracts your love. Does it expand your feeling of awareness, or does it contract it?

Look for those energies. If it expands your love and your feeling of awareness, then listen further. If it contracts them, we would back away.

The next point: How do you handle these intrusions? Always surround yourself in White Light. Oh, we know that's old-fashioned. White Light has been around "forever!" But we suggest it's a very powerful energy, and that as you always surround yourself in the White Light, you can more readily and easily handle "unwanted entities."

Call upon what we call your Higher Self. Call upon that channeled energy to make sure that the energy is pure and clean. Also, you can call upon God, upon God/Goddess/All That Is. That's what your spirituality is about — having a living, breathing, loving, embracing relationship with a God/Goddess/All That Is that's real, that's part of your life — not some abstraction way out there that you can't possibly relate to, but something that's real. Call upon that force, that power, to keep it clear, to keep it clean.

Finally, we would suggest to check your motivation. "Why am I doing this?"

We know it has become very popular to say, "Don't ask why. Don't ask why. Asking why takes you away from your experience." That is when you ask "the why for explanation." When you ask "the why for understanding," it gives you back your power. Therefore, many have suggested "don't ask why," and, in fact, they have given up their power in doing so.

Ask why. Oh, please, ask why over and over again, and don't settle for anything less than understanding.

Ask: "What am I doing here? I'm wanting to channel this energy. Why? Why do I want to channel this energy? To impress my friends? To be the hottest thing at the next party? To make a bunch of bucks? What is my motivation? Is it to learn? Is it to expand? Is it to stretch? Is it to become more of who I am?"

If you will be very honest with yourself (and ultimately you will be … ultimately you'll never lie, ultimately … ultimately), if you will go ahead and jump the gun on that and just start out telling the truth, it can help you.

Anonymous Question, Los Angeles Whole Life Expo, 1987

Q: What steps can a person take if he or she would like to channel an entity? Is that something that is really safe or appropriate for anyone to do?

Lazaris: What's the best way to channel an entity? To that extent, we would answer the question two ways.

If you're looking for an external entity, someone who is objectively separate from you, or if you are looking for some sort of consciousness for the purposes of interacting in an external fashion, we do not encourage you. Some can channel an objective and separate entity. That kind of channeling — where the purpose or the intent is to have the energy interact with other people — we do not encourage people to try to develop it. If it is going to happen, it will happen without conscious development.

"I'd like to channel an entity today and start a new career tomorrow." It can be dangerous for a person to sit down and decide, "Gee, I'd like to channel an entity, and it's a new career and a way to make some money."

If anything happens, most likely what you're going to get is a lower astral entity, as we would call it, usually a trickster, someone who might give you valuable information just long enough to get you hooked, and then start giving you a bunch of misinformation or just totally nonsensical information to make you feel totally useless, worthless, and impotent.

Also, your own negative ego in its "pomp and circumstance" can mimic so as to appear to be some sort of a higher entity. Or, you can get disincarnate consciousnesses who have no particular grand wisdom of any sort whatever, but who can offer their quite personal and quite bigoted opinions rather readily.

Therefore, you can channel a very polluted sort of energy, and a very dangerous energy. That can be a problem.

Classical or objective entity channeling does occur, of course. However, it develops naturally. You don't seek it; it finds you.

However, if you want to channel yourself, if you want to get in touch with an aspect of your counselors, your guides or guardians, if you want to get in touch with your Higher Self for your own personal growth, we would encourage that. "I want to be able to channel an energy of help, love, and divinity. I want to be able to touch into that energy for my own personal growth, for my own personal expansions." We encourage that very nicely, absolutely. Therefore, such development can take place.

The key to it is to be very clear on your motivation. Why? Why do I want to do this? To help myself? To make my life happier? To bring me closer to my own source of being? To bring me closer to God/Goddess/ All That Is, to bring me closer to the Source, to help me grow, to expand, to make my life more pleasant and more beneficial for me and those around me? To bring greater value?

There are any number of beautiful and powerful reasons to be channeling in that capacity. If a person is very clear on their intent, then we suggest through various processes and meditations — whichever works the most appropriately, Eastern or Western, active or passive — you can open yourself up. Basically, it is not to "surrender" in the traditional religious sense of giving your life over, but to "surrender" in the sense of opening yourself up, of allowing a certain energy to communicate through you. Indeed you can develop along those lines.

Many artists, whether they're painters, writers, composers, or artists in any number of capacities, know very well that when they're in the midst of the creative process they are channeling. Basically what they're doing is

— and therefore the basic sense of channeling is — getting out of the way.

The painter, in that sense, lets the paint and the canvas interact. The writer allows the words and the blank paper to have an embracing relationship. The composer lets the notes and the score talk together without impeding, without impinging, without forcing his own or her own activities upon it. They let themselves become a channel for that interaction. Then the end result can happen very beautifully.

To develop subjective personal channeling you have to be well-motivated. Also, you have to be willing to get out of the way. You have to be willing to let the ideas, the consciousness, and the love interact directly with reality. You must be willing to be a conduit. As you will do that, then you can channel — for yourself, not necessarily for the world, not necessarily for independent or separate clients.

We had someone tell us once, "Hey, I began channeling. Lazaris, I began channeling. Do you think I can make a lot of money out of it?" And we said, "No, we're sorry, but we don't think so, particularly not with that attitude and with that outlook."

Similarly, as we suggest, everybody can learn to draw, but not everybody is going to be a great artist. We encourage people to draw. We encourage people to write. Also, we encourage people to recognize that they may not put together the Great American Novel, and they may not put together some masterpiece. They can enjoy themselves and learn from their own process of creativity privately. And that, we sense, is very beautiful and very appropriate.

David Rogers, **Llewellyn's New Times,** *St. Paul, Minnesota*

Lazaris: Oh, please, we wish they would! We talk to people in that sense about counselors, for example. We call them counselors. Others call them guardian angels or guides. Various terms have been used. Every one of you has at least two counselors, one represented in the male form, and one represented in the female form. There are at least two, and there can be more.

Q: Is it appropriate for people to do their own channeling, to try and tap into their own higher spiritual entity?

In fact, you have a whole panoply of what we call the "Unseen Friends." You have a Child, first of all, that is not just a circle on a blackboard in a Transactional Analysis model of communication, but is a very living, breathing aspect of yourself. You have a Child, and an Adolescent. You have a grown-up in there that's a parenting part of yourself. You have counselors, as we say. Similarly, there is a Future Self whom you are becoming. There is a Higher Self. There is a relationship that we encourage people to have with a sense of God/Goddess/All That Is that is very personal. It is not with the totality of God/Goddess/All That Is, but with an aspect of that Source with whom you can interact personally and privately.

We encourage you to turn inward, to go into meditation, to talk to your counselors, to talk to your Inner Child. Talk to these parts of yourself. Ask them questions. Get their input. Get information. This is channeling. It's internalized, most definitely.

Some people find that they can externalize this channeling process. Within all the creative arts there are those who, while caught in the wonder and the flow of the process of creating, feel like they are channeling. Outside the creative arts, you may have found yourself thinking or talking spontaneously only to discover beautiful new information that makes you wonder, "Where did that come from?"

This is what we call Subjective Channeling, where you can channel for yourselves to add to your own lifestyle. We encourage you to seek this kind of channeling. Subjective Channeling is primarily internal and can be very helpful in your growth. It is also available to anyone who really desires to develop it.

Then there is what we'd call the Objective Channeling, which is what the Channel does, which is what the one who is called Jach does. You see, we are not his teacher. He has his own counselors, his own teachers, his own Future Self, etc. We indeed help out, certainly so, but we're not specifically his counselor or guide or guardian angel, or whatever. He subjectively channels them for himself, so to speak, to seek guidance in that way.

He does talk to us as well. However, we channel through information not just for him and not just for his own benefit, but also for the benefit of the people with whom we talk.

Therefore, Objective Channeling as opposed to Subjective Channeling is something that is not universally available. Everybody can draw, but only certain people are artists. Everyone can write, but only certain people are novelists. Similarly, we suggest, everyone can channel to a certain degree, but not everybody wants to, or is willing to, or is able to channel in this objective way. Not everyone can reach vast varieties of people with their vast varieties of concerns.

Objective Channeling is something that comes more naturally to some. It just opens up in some and never will in others.

Brian Enright/Lisa Michelle Guest, **Los Angeles &**
Orange County Resources, *Los Angeles*

Channeling & Personal Growth

Lazaris: It's a multiple role. Part of the message of channeling is a message of discernment, clearly so. You know, for example, in your practices and the study of meditation, there are all kinds of meditative procedures out there, all kinds of people teaching meditation. Some of them are very good. Some of them ... ah, well, a little nebulous at best ... and some, quite frankly, aren't doing a very good job at all.

You know that meditation isn't just meditation. You hear: "Meditation is meditation is meditation — it doesn't matter." Yes, it *does* matter! There are ways, appropriate ways, and not-so-appropriate ways.

Channeling has gone through the same sort of thing. At one time people felt that a channeled entity was just a channeled entity was just a channeled entity. It didn't matter. "They must be telling the truth because ..." There is no way you can say that just because it's channeled it's true and that you don't have to question it, that you don't have to wonder about it, that you don't have to apply it, that you don't have to make your own decisions.

Many people wanted that. They wanted channeling to be the panacea. "Here's some entity from other levels who's going to give me all the answers and is going to make my life work. All I have to do is to listen to everything they say and just have faith in it."

People have been hurt rather sadly and have been misled and mistaught. Entities on other levels have to be taken as you take people. You first have to learn, and you need to discern, and you need to decide whether it

Q: In an overall sense, could you tell me what role you see being played by channeling in regard to spiritual evolution on Earth?

works for you. Part of the message of channeling is to discern.

Additionally, the role of channeling is a teaching role, but it is not something that is the final answer. It provides an avenue of growth. It provides an opportunity.

"Your world is ready to grow, to change — very rapidly, very powerfully, very beautifully."

We'll be the first to say, for example, that we are not for everybody. There are some people who will not allow themselves to benefit from what we have to say. There are too many obstacles and beliefs that would get in their way. The very *fact* of our existence might get in the way. It's just too difficult for some people.

Others might project father — they might want to make us into a father, or make us into some sort of guru, or master, or some sort of god that knows every answer, and they might want to hang on our every word. No. We maybe can't be of benefit to those people, either.

Channeling is a tool, an avenue, and for many it will be a tremendously valuable tool that will allow them catapulting levels of growth, sensationally, wonderfully. For others it will not be the avenue at all, and therefore we say, "If it's for you, get involved. If it's not, then don't and don't feel you should just because your friends are. If this kind of teaching works for you, it works; if it doesn't, it doesn't."

Thirdly, it's a time that people are wanting to grow, and they're opening themselves up and inviting more and more opportunity. Those entitites who are honestly channeling valuable information are not necessarily the "answer," as we say. They offer an accelerated opportunity of growth. They are one of many opportunities. The channeling phenomenon has a message: "Your world is ready to grow, to change — very rapidly, very powerfully, very beautifully."

The channeling process, which has been going on for thousands upon thousands of years without much publicity, is now again being used, and it provides an opportunity for people to augment their growth because you, as a civilization, are ready to grow. You are seeking answers that traditional spiritual avenues are simply not providing — that traditional Eastern or traditional Western methods are not providing — and therefore you are seeking new, different, and innovative answers to the questions that you have been asking for so very long.

You're ready to grow. You're wanting to grow. And you're ready to open up to as many different avenues as possible.

Lee Perry, Van Nuys, California

Lazaris: Just because someone is coming from a level that is not physical, for whatever reason — because they've passed beyond that physical plane or they've never been there — just because they're talking to you does not necessarily mean that they have anything of value to say. That is very true.

Q: Why is it that someone who's never been physical would have a better knowledge of the physical plane than someone here?

As an analogy: It all depends upon where you stand on the hill. And therefore, those that are standing fairly low on the hill, in the valley, for example, can perhaps tell the truth of what they sense, but their view is limited, their scope is limited. The further they move up the hill, the grander a view they have. When you reach high up on the hill, then you have great vistas of information, great vistas of understanding. Just as with human beings, where there is a variance in the degree of one's knowledge, so with entities there's such a variance, absolutely.

Why is our insight perhaps more helpful? Well, in our own experience, we do not have time, and therefore we can grasp a sense of what you call your past along with what you call your present and your future, and therefore we can perhaps offer a perspective that is different than the perspective you would normally hold.

Through the interaction between you and us, in our talking together, our perception and your perception can blend together to create an alchemy out of which can come something that is grander than either your perception or our perception alone. Therefore, we are offering that help.

Because we are not part of your set (in the sense that we are not part of the set of that which has ever been physical), we are not so limited by those beliefs, those prejudices or those particular attitudes. We can offer a different and sometimes more helpful insight into how *your* set works.

Indeed, if you look at mathematical theory, and set theory most particularly, the truth of the matter is this: As long as you are a part of a set, you cannot fully understand that set. The only way that you can fully understand and comprehend a set is to move outside it.

Therefore, we are outside of your set and therefore have an opportunity to understand your reality perhaps more precisely and more clearly than you can. We can perhaps pass that knowledge on to you so that you might combine it with what you believe, with what your attitudes are, with the feelings and thoughts that you hold, and with the choices and decisions that you have been making so that you can make them more clearly, or at least more consciously. If, indeed, that is what happens, then we feel that our work, our inter-action, our communication has been complete.

Brian Enright/Lisa Michelle Guest, **Los Angeles &**
Orange County Resources, *Los Angeles*

The New Age

Lazaris: Indeed, there are a number of differences. Perhaps a bit of a preamble ... There are certain ancient principles that are part of your mystical history from the beginnings of time that are true. They are the core, the backbone, of all mysticism. Therefore, Old or New, they will be there. There are also remembrances of times past, remembrances of knowledges that you once had from advanced civilizations, and from unconscious memory between lifetimes. They will also be part of a core of the New Age just as they are part of the core of the Old Age.

Q: **What is the difference between the New Age and the Old Age?**

Many will say there's nothing new in the New Age. That is not true. Some will say that the New Age is just the Old Age remembered. Perhaps that is a nicer way of saying it, but nonetheless it is not totally true.

There is something very new in the New Age. What is new is the fact that power is now conscious. You see, initially power was seated in your Higher Conscious Mind where you were but puppets, where you were but marionettes of the puppeteer. Everything was done for you. Everything was taken care of. Power was in the

Higher Conscious Mind, but you weren't conscious of it, and therefore you were not responsible for it.

It was the time that Biblically is referred to as the Garden of Eden, where life was innocent and blissful, where there was no responsibility. There was no knowledge of good and bad. There was no decision making. There were no choices or decisions. There were no thoughts or feelings that were personal, individual. Certainly there were no positions of attitude or belief that could be definitely identified as personal and private.

"You make conscious decisions. Everything you do is a conscious decision. That you pretend it isn't, that you look the other way, that you put those conscious decisions in some sort of automatic relationship does not make them unconscious or subconscious. They're still conscious."

The myths of all religions begin with this "time of innocence" because there are certain unconscious — not subconscious, but unconscious — remembrances of that time when power was seated in the Higher Consciousness without responsibility. That power moved into the unconscious mind, where indeed human beings moved from that state of bliss, that innocence of childhood, into a world where they could distinguish right from wrong. They didn't always know what to do with it, but they could distinguish it.

Therefore, the instinctive world of "knee-jerk response" began. The instinctive world of "fight or flight" began, a world where human beings were not really human beings but more like human animals. People existed in that very primitive and very rough state — a very "cave man" sort of energy that you read about or think about. Again, from your unconscious memory it seems very right and very real to you.

This was a time of instinct, a time when power was instinctive. There was a little more responsibility, because you knew the difference between right and wrong, good and bad, healthy and not healthy, but you didn't really have the full responsibility for your life or your world.

Power then moved from the unconscious to the subconscious mind. That's what Freud described, suggesting that motivation came from childhood experience, that you could discover it through dreams and altered states and through psychoanalysis — that indeed there was an *id* and a *libido* and various other components of the subconscious self. The subconscious self directed your life. The reason you did the things you did was because of your subconscious programming. It was so automatic. Based upon your past, based upon what you had gone through, based upon the trauma of those experiences, you were motivated.

Freud was quite correct, but he came in at the tail end of that period of time, when the consciousness had already moved. Now, more clearly than ever, it is moving — because the transition is not a rapid thing — from the subconscious to the conscious.

Once one could legitimately say, "Ah, that was subconscious. I didn't know I was doing it. That was a subconscious motivation. I was totally oblivious to it." Now, more and more, those statements cannot be made, because power is conscious.

You make conscious decisions. Everything you do is a conscious decision. That you pretend it isn't, that you look the other way, that you put those conscious decisions in some sort of automatic relationship does not make them unconscious or subconscious. They're still conscious.

The New Age is the age when people become conscious — where indeed power is conscious — where you create your own reality, where you create your own reality individually and then collectively — and where the future is not determined by pre-destined patterns. The future is not determined by the predictors from the past, but rather is determined by conscious choice. Now that is quite a marvelous, incredible reality where

"What is new in the New Age, concisely, is that power is conscious and will continue to become more and more conscious."

indeed everything in your reality is more and more becoming a conscious creation.

Simple words: power is conscious. It is a tremendously important concept, however, because what it means is that all the predictions from the past are now up for grabs. All the energy of the past that determined what the future would be no longer has that kind of power. Well, you can give it power consciously, but we suggest that you have the conscious choice.

That's going to scare a lot of people. That's going to cause a lot of people to "go crazy" in their reality. They won't know how to deal with it. They won't want to deal with it. They won't want to believe it. Alas, reality will reflect it ... reality will reflect it. All that has been objective in the past — the solidness, the concreteness, the determination, the pre-destination — will become subjective, by people's choice.

What is new in the New Age, concisely, is that power is conscious and will continue to become more and more conscious. What is unique in the New Age is that more and more individuals are coming to that conclusion.

You know, thousands of years ago a person here, a person there came to that realization. They knew that power had moved from the Higher Conscious to the unconscious to the subconscious, and they took back their power. They took it back consciously, and for them the New Age began at that time.

Perhaps the New Age began for certain Lemurians, if you accept that reality, and there were perhaps Atlantineans who came to the understanding of the New Age. Throughout your modern world, the world subsequent to those realities, individuals here and there, in groups of two or three, came to this understanding. And their New Age began then. It's a personal process.

But now in your world, more individuals are experiencing their personal process. That personal process is becoming a massive movement of energy, and that is what the New Age is about.

Mary Pratt/Jack Clarke, **New Age Information Network,** *Atlanta*

azaris: First of all they're both seeking a sense of spirituality. We suggest that whether that religion is Fundamentalist, traditional, or even *avante garde* in its approaches, it has in common a seeking, a seeking of God — or as we call it God/Goddess/All That Is.

Q: What are the similarities between religion and metaphysics?

Metaphysics similarly involves seeking that same feeling of spirituality, that same energy, that same Light. They call it by different names, and they look on different paths, but they are seeking the same energy and the same Light.

Secondly, both attempt to deal with the issue of responsibility. Some Fundamentalist approaches try to shift the majority of that responsibility off onto God. But most Fundamentalist, traditional, and even *avante garde* religions, as they exist today, at least try to take some level of responsibility for the reality they create. They suggest that one's happiness and one's light are somehow connected to one's involvement in spirituality. Thus, you are responsible for your happiness. The more spiritual you are, the happier you will be.

The metaphysical approach is to suggest that you are totally responsible for the reality that you are creating, either by causing or allowing that reality creation. There is a semblance of understanding that the more one is involved in one's spirituality, the more one is involved in one's search for God/Goddess/All That Is, the more positive, the more successful life will be. Those similarities also exist.

Thirdly, there is a moral code that both rather suggest. There is a level of integrity, a level of impeccability that both put forth.

Whether you believe in the particular codes that either put forth, at least they both have a sense of that morality, a sense of that integrity, a sense of that impeccability. They each have a standard, a code, that a person can follow, by necessity within the more Fundamentalist/traditional approaches or by preference in the more metaphysical approaches — but nonetheless there is that code.

Fourthly, both believe in Love and the power of that Love. They both believe in the power of positive energy and in the power of God or God/Goddess/All That Is (in the case of metaphysics).

And so we sense that although there are differences, certainly so, there are some areas in which the two are very much the same.

*Betty Finas, **Golden Braid Books Newsletter**, Salt Lake City*

Lazaris: Well, not a merging as you would think of it. No. There will be no organizational merging. There is a dichotomy between metaphysics and Fundamentalist and traditional religions that look upon this New Spirituality, as we call it (which is more than a New Age), as something evil, something bad, something terrible. They see metaphysics as a replacement, and therefore they fear it.

Q: Do you think there will ever be a merging of organized religion with what I would call enlightened thinking or New Age thinking?

The New Spirituality — the New Age — is not a replacement, but an extension, an expansion beyond that which organized religions believe. The New Spirituality builds upon many of the traditional religious ideals, principles and values.

These misconceptions and the fear that they produce lead to the commonly accepted polarity between religion and new thought. This polarity is normally seen as a left-right division.

There's an additional polarity between the top and the bottom. There are those within the New Age Movement that speak positively and beautifully of a future that can come. There are those within the traditional religions and the Fundamentalist religions — televangelists as they may be — that speak similarly of the positive and the potential future that humankind can create. There are within that Fundamentalist religion the negative soothsayers that speak only of the doom and the horror and the gnashing of teeth, just as there are those on the metaphysical side that can only talk of Doom and Gloom and the end of the world.

There is not only the division left and right, but also the division top and bottom, and these metaphysicians that speak positively of the hopes of mankind and these Christians who speak similarly are in greater alliance with each other than they are with their respective metaphysicians and Christians who think, speak and act negatively. Though this alliance will never be verbally spoken or officially named, in the hearts and minds it is there.

There will be that time in the future when these two groups will be more aligned than they've ever been and saying basically, "We're going to lead this world into that Age, into that newness, into that possibility that we both, from our different perspectives, and with our different vernaculars, see." We suggest that is going to occur in this time period that is to come.

The Complete Guide to Channeling, a video produced by Penny Price Productions, Pacific Palisades

With love and peace ...

Lazaris

Women, Men & Sexuality

The Differences between and the Needs of Men and Women
The Emergence of Feminine Energy
The Femininity/Power/Success Matrix of Women
Sexuality & Spirituality

Q: Although we may be androgynous in essence, it is obvious that when we come into bodies we choose one of two types — male or female. From the view-point of one's spiritual growth, how do the needs differ be-tween men and women, or are there any differen-ces?

Lazaris: Obviously, as a Spark of Consciousness, there is no sex, there is no division. But each life-time you do choose a particular energy pattern that you are to focus on. The obvious goal, in that sense, is to become whole. Therefore, as you begin a particular path in your spirituality, each lifetime is its own unique segment of the path. So, you begin from a particular standpoint and a particular attitude, a particular angle which does differ between men and women. There are differences in terms of their needs.

When it comes to the end of it, however, when a man or a woman reaches that state of wholeness, then there is no difference. So, perhaps, one takes a temporary de-tour through that which is maleness or a temporary de-tour through that which is femaleness to end up in that state of wholeness.

What are those differences? Well, "man energy" and "woman energy" are not really the appropriate divi-sions, because not all men are just masculine and not all women are just feminine. Therefore, the division should be drawn between masculine energy and feminine energy. Most women emphasize the feminine energy. Most men emphasize the masculine energy. All people are trying to become both.

For women, first of all, spirituality has to have what we call a Sacred Setting. If you will work with the Sacred Setting, with creating environment, with creat-ing an attitude, with creating an energy field as you move into your spiritual endeavors, you will benefit greatly and will step in lightly.

Now, why is this? First of all, feminine energy is far more adept at creating a setting, far more adept at creating the space which the form is going to take, into which the content is going to come. Therefore, it is valuable for a woman to begin her spiritual endeavor —

whether it is alone in a meditative process or in a group effort of women coming together to share and to love and to grow as women — by creating the Sacred Setting, by creating an environment that is conducive to safety, that is conducive to growth.

Men, on the other hand, don't create that setting. It's not that they don't need it; they just don't create it. They rely upon the feminine side of themselves and rely upon women to create that Sacred Setting. Once the space is created, they need to responsibly fill that space with enlightening content.

The second thing which is important is that women need to be aware of their power, and they need to open up to discovering the power of being women — not the power given to them by men, but the power that they have innately because of who they are. Men don't need to be awakened to this in the same way, because they are already conditioned to believe they are power-ful. Men need to learn what power is.

Women know what power is intuitively. So, there-fore, women need to *accept* power. Men need to learn about power. Women need to create the Sacred Setting. Men need to create the time and the space for their spiritual endeavors.

Thirdly, women need to come to a greater sense of their own identity. Women need not only to accept their power, they also need to find and accept their identity.

To digress: Years ago women were allowed only to be feminine, to be homemakers. Every woman should be married by the time she was 18 or 19 or, if she went to college, by age 21. She should start having children at least by age 23 or 24. If something was wrong, well, maybe then in her late 20s. But she should have at least two or three, maybe even four, children (two boys and two girls), and that is what a woman was. That's what men gave her permission to do and be. She could work during the War, but once it was over, "go home." The men came home. "Give them back the jobs that are rightfully and honestly theirs, and go back to your kitchens, back to your homes." That was the way it was.

But women said, "No, we want something else." And who did they go to? They went to the men and said, "Men, give us our rights."

Now that's crazy. The women then went to the men and said, "OK, men, you're not more powerful than we are. You're not the lawmakers here. We are just as equal as you are. You better give us permission to be as equal as you."

The men said, "Hmmm. We'll think about it." And the women said, "We're going to fight." And they burned their bras.

Then the men came back and they said, "OK, women, we're going to give you permission to be powerful, but the price you must pay for it is that you have to choose: You're either going to be feminine (wrapped up in cellophane with a martini when I get home) or you're going to be free and, therefore, dress like me, act like me, think like me — that's your permission! You cannot be feminine *and* powerful. You can be feminine *or* powerful." And most women said, "Fine," and thought they were liberated.

Now women who are part of the New Consciousness are saying, "Wait a minute. We made a big mistake years ago. We should never have asked men for our power, because they didn't have it in the first place. They didn't have the permission to give it to us. We should have asked ourselves for our power back. We screwed up. OK, we can correct that. We asked them, and they gave us permission to be feminine *or* to be powerful, and we thought that was liberation. We know now that it's not. What we have to do is give ourselves permission to be both powerful and feminine."

Now, what this is all getting to is that women need to turn to women, not to men, for their identity. There is a phrase out in your world, and it is so sad. "Gee, she's so great! She thinks like a man!" This is still considered a compliment. That should be the grandest insult. If a man says that to a woman, she should slap him across the face, for that is the most insulting thing to say to her.

Imagine the comment in reverse. Go up to a man that you consider powerful, or go up to a male co-worker and say, "You're so great! You think just like a woman!" What will happen to you?

You laugh, nervously, even at the thought. To think like, to act like, to be like a woman is considered an insult. Sadly, it is considered an insult even when you are speaking to a woman.

To say, "Wow, you're really fantastic! This woman thinks like a woman!" OK, now there's a compliment. That's something to be proud of. That's what we mean by getting the identity from themselves and their meaning and their power from themselves and from each other. As a spiritual group, women need to turn to women to get their identity, to get their power, to accept the power that is innately theirs, to set the Sacred Setting for what spirituality really is.

Men, on the other hand, need to create the time and the space, as we say. They need to learn what power is. Men need to turn to their own feminine energy. We're not saying become wimps. We're not saying become little boys. We're saying, in fact, become real men.

Men need to turn to their feminine energy to discover the identity of what the Goddess is, of what the

" ... women need to turn to women, not to men, for their identity.

"'She thinks like a man!' This is still considered a compliment. That should be the grandest insult."

feminine diety, that feminine aspect of the Whole Diety, is. They need to discover that particular side of themselves to gain a perspective of an identity that has hitherto been pushed and shoved and twisted by the mass consciousness.

We feel a tremendous empathy for women who turn to men for their power, who confine themselves. We see so many women who are brilliant and who are successful. They have everything except a man. Therefore, they discount their car, their friends, their home, their money, their intelligence, their spirituality. They discount it all because they don't have a man. We feel a tremendous compassion for these women along that entire spectrum.

But we also see men who have been battered by the Collective Unconscious, men who have been stripped of their masculinity, and instead have been given a bravado of machismo. You see, men who are stripped of their feelings, men who are told they shouldn't feel, that they can only be angry, and who are given a robot-like success image of what they have to become — we see them as hurting, just like the women who hurt. The way out is for them to turn to the feminine energy within them and say, "No, I am not going to be hurt by the mass consciousness. I am not going to be stripped of what is real power and be given instead a facsimile. I will not settle for shallow, robot-like machismo."

"We also see ... men who have been stripped of their masculinity, and instead have been given a bravado of machismo."

Therefore, men need to create the time and space and come to understand what power is, perhaps for the first time. They need to turn to the feminine side, to turn to the Goddess energy to clarify their own identity — not to find their identity, but to clarify their identity. They need to turn to themselves and to women. Men need to turn to men and women — not just women, not just men — to find their perspective, their identity, to fulfill their spirituality.

These are the differences. Who took the tougher road? It balances out. Most women came in with the idea that they wanted to deal with oppression, and the guaranteed way to do that is to be born in the USA. One guaranteed way to learn to deal with oppression is to be born female in the USA. Men, in that sense, came in to deal with power.

Women came in to deal with the matrix of what we call femininity, power, and success, to try to create the balance: "I can have femininity, power and success." Men came in to deal with being misled and to re-guide themselves into the true sense of masculinity, into the true sense of what it is to be a man.

When a man is an unconscious man, he is either a bore or a wimp, totally ineffectual, sitting around doing nothing with his life, and always *in potentia* — "someday, someday." When a man will break out of that mass consciousness and really discover his man-hood, really discover that it is all right to be a man, then he can stop "attacking" women and start working with them. He can truly embrace a woman — not sexually embrace — but embrace her as a real person, a friend, a consciousness. It is a beautiful, beautiful consciousness that is a real man.

Similarly, when a woman will step outside of the oppression, accept the power that is naturally hers, gain her identity from women and turn inward for who she really is, giving herself permission to be a spiritual being, then is born a real woman, a whole figure who is powerful enough to create her reality in a tender and loving way, to love her reality creatively.

There are bubbles of consciousness here and there, sparks of consciousness that are real men and real women, and when you come across them, they are wonders to behold. As you become one you become absolutely fascinating, credibly fascinating with your spirituality and with your relationship to what your spirituality is with God/Goddess/All That Is, or whatever you call the Deity.

*Krysta Gibson, **The Seattle New Times & Spiritual Women's Times**,*
Seattle, Washington

Q: Could you comment on women coming into positions of power right now? We are seeing more of them in the leadership positions and in positions where they're making changes and major policy decisions.

Lazaris: Well, what fascinates us is that as of September, 1987, women became the majority of your population. Over the next many years, with the numbers of female children being born and the whole census activity, women will continue to be the majority of the population. We find this very fascinating because one might think and assume initially that that would mean more feminine energy, right?

Do not be misled or fool yourself into thinking that females *ipso facto* have some sort of corner on feminine energy. We would suggest here that they are consciousnesses, they are sparks of consciousness, as we say, who have chosen to come into this physical life indeed to develop that feminine energy more overtly and to have access to learning about their own feminine energy more clearly. But men also have feminine energy. However, with the population increase in women and with more women "coming into positions of power," there is more awareness of feminine energy.

As these various women open up to their own feminine energy, as they stop mimicking men and their ideas of what it is to be a success, some interesting changes can occur. Women can start creating their own imagery of what it is to be a success rather than cloning men.

What happens now is that a lot of women look out there in the world and say, "I'm going to be successful," and so they learn to think like a man, act like a man, function like a man, even dress like a man — almost. Their tie is tied in a bow rather than a Windsor knot, but most women tend to measure their success in terms of how much they can be like a man in a "man's world."

This is hardly a liberating thought at all. Perhaps it would be wiser for women to start looking at being able to think like a woman and act like a woman and dress like a woman — whatever that means to her (not by anybody else's standard, but by her own) — and to start creating new pictures, new patterns, new energies of what it is to be a woman.

Even more importantly than that is to be in touch with the feminine energy. With the majority of people being women, and with more of those women coming into positions of power over the next 20 years, it will increase the awareness of the feminine energy.

Both men and women need to stop and make an evaluation of that energy because it is that feminine energy that is the creative energy, that is the nurturing energy, that is the energy that brings balance, and the energy that brings perception. The qualities of creativity, nurturing, balance and perception are the qualities that your world needs most of all, over these next 20 years, in order to Dream the solutions to the problems that seem ever-present.

Q: So we're creating our own new role models.

Lazaris: We would hope so! Yes. A lot of women are battling right now with a particular circumstance which we call the femininity matrix, which basically has three components to it: One is success. One is power. And one is femininity.

You see, many years ago, as women, you were given permission to be feminine. That's all. You couldn't be powerful. You couldn't be successful. All you had a right to be was to be feminine, and that's it.

Then the Women's Liberation Movement came along. At various stages it began and was thwarted, and began and was thwarted once again. But when it really got rolling, a group of women, separately and together, rather went out and said, "Look, we want to be liberated. We want to be free of this chauvinism, free of this male domination." Then they went to the men and said, "We want to be liberated. Is that OK?" And the men said, "Sure, you can now be feminine or powerful, but you cannot be both, and you still cannot be totally successful." And women went away thinking they'd won a grand victory. "Men have given us permission to be feminine *or* powerful."

They divided themselves between those two groups. One group of women basically said, "Our role is to be feminine, and we should become the 'Total Woman,' become totally feminine." Other women said, "No, that's somehow anti-woman; that's somehow anti-political. We want to become totally powerful and forget the femininity, forget those qualities that used to be called 'being a woman.' Let's just be powerful." And so the two camps were divided.

What's happening now is that more and more women such as yourselves, and women in the particular age group as yourself, are realizing: "Wait a minute. I don't want to have to choose between one or the other. I want to be both. In fact, not only do I want to be powerful, I want to be feminine, and I also want to be successful."

The problem is that there are very few role models. There are a number of models of what it is to be feminine, and there are a number of models of what it is to be powerful — but there are very few models of what it is to be both. Then to be successful on top of it? Out of the question!

Some women in your world are very feminine, but they are not powerful, and they are not successful. They see themselves totally as an appendage to their husbands or to the men in their lives.

Other women see themselves totally as being powerful. They have given up on having a relationship or children and don't have a home life to speak of. They say that that's unimportant. What's important is to be a powerful political, social, or economic force in the world. These women are not successful even though they have power.

Most women are not successful. They have what we call secondary success. They can have success up to a point, up to a level. But they can't really be totally successful. Oh, she may get a promotion, and she may be a vice-president, but we would suggest here she'll never be president. She'll never reach the top of the ladder, unless she forms her own company. Even then the success she has is secondary success. Most women still feel, in a rather automatic way, that the success they're entitled to is secondary — that a man is entitled to primary success.

"What is important is this: Do you love? If the answer is 'yes,' you are growing spiritually. If the answer is 'no,' you are not."

Women are "spinning plates" of power and femininity. Many of them get powerful for awhile, and jeopardize their love and their relationships — the tenderness in their life — and therefore give up the power in favor of that gentleness, that tenderness. However, now women are trying to balance those two. They are trying to keep both plates spinning. Now they want to "add a third plate," so to speak, a third plate to keep spinning, and that is: "I'm not going to settle for secondary success. I want primary success."

This is a New Age movement of energy, and a lot of women have this new matrix as their focus. A lot of women are trying not only to balance but also to increase their sphere of influence to include success in a primary way. It's very exciting.

*Cindy Saul, **PhenomeNEWS**, Southfield, Michigan*

Q: Would a higher entity discriminate against someone's sexuality?

Lazaris: Oh, clearly not. Sadly, chauvinism is rampant with mystical teachers who feel that women are less than, and that if you're really evolved, you're going to reincarnate as a male because men are better than — more evolved than — women. In truth you're a consciousness. You're a Spark of Light. You choose to be a man or a woman. You choose what race you're going to be, for whatever advantage.

You also choose a sexual preference. The point is you're in life to love. It doesn't matter who. And no highly valued consciousness would say, "Homosexuality is wrong in itself."

Perverse sexual behavior, homosexual or heterosexual, can be hurtful to your growth. It might be advisable to change your patterns, but not your preferences. Many people who choose homosexuality are choosing so to come into society and deal with oppression, just as many women do. Therefore, it can be more than all right. It can be a very valuble tool.

Craig Lee, LA Weekly, Los Angeles

Lazaris: Well, first of all, to say that *who* one loves — what sex you prefer — has any impact upon one's spirituality is absolutely ridiculous. It's crass. It's unenlightened. We feel compassion for people who sincerely believe that way, for indeed they have shut off so much of their own potential. We don't judge them as being bad or wrong. We feel compassion for them.

It is really hurtful to put forth such a statement, because there will be those who are Lesbians and Gay men who will believe it. This we see as a grand tragedy in this field of metaphysics. There are those who put themselves forth as authorities, and then they offer such bigotry, such limited and narrow-minded thought — thought which simply cannot be true.

First of all, once you move beyond the physical plane, you lose your gender. You move into the "concept" of gender on the Astral Plane. Yes, people do have male and female bodies on the Astral Plane, but they lose the gender. They hang onto the concept of gender.

On the Causal Plane, there's also the concept of gender, but once you reach the mental plane, even the concept of gender is so vague and so limited that it's barely there at all. Once you move beyond that, there's no gender whatsoever, so how can one say that homosexuality — Lesbian or Gay — is wrong or bad? Only the limited Lower World could even begin to make such judgments.

Q: Although most metaphysical groups and teachers say they espouse and teach non-judgmentalism, there are those who seem to pass judgment on homosexuals and Lesbians by stating that those who engage in same-sex relationships cannot become enlightened, cannot be spiritual. The message sometimes seems to be that heterosexuality is the preferred path for spiritual growth. What do you have to say on the subject?

Secondly, God/Goddess/All That Is sees you as Sparks of Consciousness. They don't sense your gender, even though you do. They are not impressed with your gender, you know. Unfortunately, most of you are. When they see two lights merging, that is love. They don't check gender and look under the covers and see what equipment you have. Notice we don't say "do have" and "don't have." It is very chauvinistic to suggest some have equipment and some don't. Everybody has equipment. God/Goddess/All That Is doesn't care what it is, and spiritually speaking, you shouldn't, either. Of course, you have preferences, and you should enjoy those preferences.

One can be homosexual, whether male or female, and be just as wholly and totally and completely evolved as one who chooses to be heterosexual.

What is the definition of homosexuality? It is a sexual preference. Heterosexuality is also a sexual preference — not an obligation. Therefore, a person, heterosexual or homosexual, is expressing a preference.

What is important is this: Do you love? If the answer is "yes," you are growing spiritually. If the answer is "no," you're not. Who you love has nothing to do with it. So therefore, to any Gays or Lesbians reading this we would say this: We know you've heard that you can't evolve, or that you can't be as evolved as others. When you hear this kind of limited message, use it as a signal that the speaker putting forth this "knowledge" should not be taken seriously about this particular knowledge, or perhaps about other "knowledge," either.

Lazaris: We wanted to share this because we know that throughout metaphysics it has been suggested by some people that there is a difference in spiritual potential between heterosexuals and homosexuals. And now with AIDS, there are those who are claiming a spiritual evolvement who are making irresponsible statements about AIDS being God's way of purging, that this is God's attack on homosexuals. With teachers who claim to be spiritual (and we are aware of one who writes a medical column!), this is grossly unfair, and to add that kind of judgment to the fear that's already there is totally unwarranted.

We are more than happy to be outspoken and to be putting it forth here that there is no evolutionary difference between homosexuals and heterosexuals. AIDS is not God's punishment of anybody. It is a message that each person — heterosexual or homosexual — is giving themselves. It has nothing to do with judgment by anyone on any level. There is no judgment on the higher levels.

Many homosexuals feel "less than." Some now have gone the other way, feeling that somehow they are "better than." Their anger and hurt have turned to militant arrogance. No. We would suggest: No. It just doesn't work that way. They are not less. They are not more. People are people. People are Sparks of Consciousness, as seen by the higher levels. The body — whether it's pretty, unattractive, tall, short, fat, skinny, preferring same sex or opposite sex — is all just part of the illusion. It matters only to those who are participating in the illusion.

*Krysta Gibson, **The Seattle New Times &
Spiritual Women's Times**, Seattle*

Q: Beautifully spoken. There will be many people reading this who will be grateful to hear your viewpoint, who will now be able to move closer to loving themselves and to loving that part of themselves which believed the untruths about sexual preference.

With Love & Peace ...

Lazaris

Discovering
God, Goddess & All That Is

The Synergy of God/Goddess/All That Is — Defining the Goddess Energy
Practical Uses of the Goddess Energy — Obstacles to Working
with the Goddess — Men and the Goddess Energy
Becoming More of God/Goddess/All That Is

Q: Lazaris, you frequently use the term God/ Goddess/All That Is.

Lazaris: Yes.

Q: Can you explain this term in further detail?

Lazaris: We know in your world you refer to "God" so much. That term has such an overlay, so many pictures from childhood that are laid on top of it. You have the image of an old man with a white beard sitting upon some sort of cloud, destroying cities when he feels like it, and doing all those dastardly things that the Old Testament rather attributes to his name. You also have all the imagery of the Crusades and everything else that is attributed to the name of Jesus in the New Testament. Your image of God is also created by all these pictures of pews too hard to sit in, and pencils too dull to draw with that are part of your childhood imagery of what God is.

So many people who are involved in the mystical/metaphysical movements of this day have moved away from that, and have wanted to move away from the conditions, the limitations, and the guilts that were imposed upon them by their childhood religions — not by God, not by Jesus, not by their sense of deity, but by the organization, by their parents, or by the system, or by the ministers, priests, or rabbis.

Many want to move away from those pictures of God. Therefore, as they move into the alternatives, many have shut God out. They shut that door completely. We want to open that door again — not the same door that you saw before, but a truer door. We want to open the door not to the God of the Bible that you think of, but to the truer, more complete God that has not been — how do you say? — edited, that has not been rewritten, that has not been translated or voted upon in those councils that were put together in the early time of your history.

Rather, we are speaking of a fuller sense of God, which is a male energy of God, but more than a male energy, it is also a feminine energy, and therefore Goddess. And more than a feminine energy, it is the synergy of God and Goddess to produce All That Is, which is more than male and more than female. There is a whole that's much greater than the sum of its parts. Rather than calling it God, or Goddess, or All That Is, we combine the three terms, God/Goddess/All That Is.

We realize that indeed that may be a little more difficult for some people to say, but anybody who has studied Eastern thought and studied with Swami Such-and-Such-and-Such-and-Such certainly is used to saying many-syllabled names. To honor the deity, or that sense of the source, by referring to it as God/Goddess/All That Is, one term, we do not feel is too much to ask. Therefore, we refer to it most clearly and most frequently in the synergistic sense of God/Goddess/All That Is, rather than in its pieces and its parts.

*Jim Faubel, **Transformation Times**, Beaver Creek, Oregon*

Q: What is your definition of the Goddess energy?

Lazaris: There is no one, all-inclusive definition. The beauty of the allure, as well as the illusiveness, of the Goddess energy is that each person must define it/Her for themselves.

What is God? What is the God energy? Everyone has an answer to that question. Even if the answer is filled with a lot of "hems" and "haws," everyone has at least some sort of answer to the question "What is God?" The definition of God ultimately — regardless of where it begins — will include such words as light, love, isness, allness, and ultimately, All That Is.

People seem satisfied with these definitions, and they should be, because it is impossible to adequately describe the omni-dimensional concept of God in a two-dimensional language such as yours. You do the best you can, and we would suggest you have done admirably well, because indeed it is true that God is light, God is love. Reality is God in action. God is All That Is.

Well, what is Goddess? What is the Goddess energy? This definition is more difficult for people. That difficulty is not an indication of ignorance, but rather an indictment of a society that is still riddled with male chauvinism. The Goddess is defined with such words as light, love, isness, allness, and All That Is. For, you see, the Goddess is also light. The Goddess is love. Reality is similarly Goddess in action. Goddess, like God, is All That Is. It would not be appropriate, though, to see the Goddess as a part of God, as some indeed would like to.

However, it is appropriate to see God and Goddess as the expressive and creative energies of a force that is greater than each. To see them as the expressive and creative energies of All That Is, is what is appropriate. You see, your paternal religions throughout the world have presented an image of the deity as being all male in the form of God, in the form of a Son, and perhaps somewhat amorphously in the form of a Holy Ghost (which would be most comparable to All That Is). You have been satisfied with this limited concept of deity, especially when you were content to give your power away to guru, master, minister, or priest.

As you have begun to take back your power, as you have begun to search and seek meaning, as you have begun perception into your own personal reality, as you have begun your own personal spiritual journey home, you have glimpsed something you hitherto did not know existed.

In your search for God, you have glimpsed the Goddess — just a tiny glimmer indeed, but a glimpse at least. That glimpse has opened a door for the emergence of the Goddess energy. More correctly, that glimpse has opened the door for the reemergence of a powerful, incredibly beautiful energy, for the reemergence of the Goddess.

As this energy reemerges, you are discovering your own definition of Goddess, as well as rediscovering a more complete and a more useful definition of God. Though there is no single definition of the Goddess energy that would be acceptable to all, there are some key principles that come close to defining that energy.

The Goddess energy is the idealized feminine energy — not the idealized woman, not the idealized female — but the idealized feminine energy. Feminine energy is truly available to all that are female, all that are women, and — this is the important part — it is also fully available to all who are male, and all who are men.

Well, what are these key principles that come the closest to defining the Goddess? They are, simply put: Imagining, Feeling, Conceiving and Perceiving.

Imagining is your ability, with eyes opened or closed, to travel thousands of miles in your mind and to experience a reality as though you were there. Imagining is your very special and unique ability to dream and to vision. Imagining is a most wondrous and powerful energy that allows you to conjure things that have never been and to walk among them touching and feeling and responding. Imagining is that special quality you have that allows you to reach into the future and to create things, ideas, feelings, and concepts, and to bring them back into your current illusion and to make them real. All of these things that are part of what is imagin-

"Imagining is a most wondrous and powerful energy that allows you to conjure things that have never been and to walk among them ... "

" ... to be able to cry and to be able to laugh, to be able to love, to be able to hate — that function within you, that ability to feel is that feminine energy."

ing are a part of that feminine principle, are a part of that feminine energy that is, indeed, available to each and every one of you.

The ability to feel ... Even when you don't know what love is, you are capable of feeling love. Even when you've never experienced sadness, you are capable of reaching deep within yourself and discovering that feeling, that sense, that energy.

That ability to look at a picture on the newsreel, or to watch a movie on television, that ability to read the newspaper or a fictionalized version of someone's story and to be able to cry and to be able to laugh, to be able to love, to be able to hate — that function within you, that ability to feel is that feminine energy. And though many of you will deny your feelings, though many of you will run from them, though many of you will try to pretend you don't have any feelings, indeed you do. It's a wondrous, powerful, and beautiful part of you that is that Goddess within.

Conceiving is one of the most misunderstood concepts related to the Goddess energy. In your world of workshops and seminars, so often people think they are coming forth with new ideas, new concepts. So often they think they are conceiving something brand new, whereas, in fact, all they're doing is taking someone else's ideas, someone else's experiences, changing them around, using a different vernacular, or adding a few of their own personalized experiences to the consensus, and then calling it new.

To go to someone's workshops and take various copious notes and then turn around and change the title, to read someone's book on how to do this or that or the other and then to outline it in a different form, may be a workable system — it may even be valuable — but do not fool yourself into thinking that you have conceived of something new. At best you have taken someone else's conception and copied, imitated, or plagiarized it, but you have not conceived of it for yourself.

Though we would not judge such copying and lifting, we would simply add that it is never fulfilling. It never gives you a true sense of your value, a true sense of your worth, a true sense of your esteem. It always ends up eventually leaving you feeling hollow and feeling empty because you aren't conceiving. You aren't giving birth to something new. No matter how many times you use the word *conceiving*, it doesn't make it so.

The other problem with this word is that people, realizing this problem we've just outlined, go to the other extreme and start talking of bizarre things that are so far-fetched, out-of-reach, and out-of-range that they have never been talked about before in the history of the human consciousness. They therefore believe: "Aha! Because I've said something that no one has ever said, because I've spoken words that have never even been uttered before, now I'm conceiving of something new!"

Once again, that you are flying far afield in delusion, in fantasy, or in a decaying dream does not make it conception. To conceive something is to reach into the very essence of your being and to find something that has never been and to give birth to it, to give birth to an idea, to give birth to a concept, to give birth to a level and an understanding of humanity that has never been before — but that does exist, that does function, that does make sense in your world.

When a woman conceives a child, the measure of her successful conception is the ability of that child to survive. When you conceive of an idea, the measure of your successful conception is, similarly, the ability of that idea to survive in your world. To come up with cockamamie ideas that are so far-fetched that they make no sense whatever is not conception: It is delusion; it is fantasy; it is perhaps the decaying dream.

"To perceive is to understand in the realms where words cannot tread, in the realms that are beyond images, beyond the words, beyond the feelings, beyond the conceptions."

The key to conception is that it is brand new and that it works. To be able to conceive is part of the feminine energy that has been lost and that now, in your late '80s and into the '90s and into the turn of the century, is once again beginning to emerge.

The fourth quality of the feminine principle and of the Goddess energy is that of perception. This word and this concept are also very misunderstood. That is a result, perhaps, of the duality in your world where there are those who are emphasizing only the intellect. Some say coming up with some sort of intellectual understanding, some sort of intellectual meaning, is all that is important. Yet others, perhaps confused and confounded, tell you to drop all your intellectualism and to go only with your feelings, only to feel what the world is about.

While one looks down their nose at those without the proper degrees and the proper credentials, the other looks down their nose at those that have them. We would suggest that both are incorrect. It is neither more valuable to think (rather than to feel) than it is to feel (rather than to think). In fact, you can't do one without doing the other. You must think in order to allow yourself to feel and to follow those feelings that many are encouraging you to do. Similarly, you must feel in order to think, in order to develop that intellect. In order to use that intellect, it must be companioned with feeling to be of any value.

Perception is something that stands outside understanding or meaning, something that stands beyond the intellectualization or the emotionalization of your world. To perceive is to step back and to take a look at the larger picture. To perceive is to allow the meanings and understandings to come to you rather than chasing after them. To perceive is to understand in the realms where words cannot tread, in the realms that are beyond the images, beyond the words, beyond the feelings, beyond the conceptions. To perceive is to approach that energy which is Goddess, that energy which is God, and that energy that is more than each, which is All That Is.

These are the qualities that best describe what is the Goddess energy. There is no one all-inclusive definition. The beauty and the allure, as well as the illusiveness, of the Goddess is that each person must both define and then discover Her for themselves.

Lazaris: We understand the question and indeed realize the importance of asking it. We also understand that over the next many years, through the turn of this century, as this energy that is the Goddess emerges and indeed reemerges, and emerges and re-emerges over and over again, individually and collectively within your consciousness, that the question will be put many times and in many ways.

Q: What would be some of the ways people could practically use this energy in their daily lives?

Even so, it does feel very strange to be auditioning the Goddess energy. To show you its practical uses before its acceptance is, in a way, trying to convince you that it's worthwhile, that it's practical, that it's worth your time and energy to stop and define and discover this most wondrous energy. How many of you would seriously ask: "What are the practical values of God in your everyday life?" It is somehow accepted that, of course, the presence of God is valuable and is important, if not indeed essential to your daily existence. It is almost as though if one must ask, one hasn't even begun to become aware of what God is.

Well, the Goddess energy really doesn't need to audition, either, but to answer the question *What are the practical and valuable uses?* we would look at some, indeed.

First, we would suggest, on a very pragmatic level, being in touch with this energy can augment your programming. The times that you go into meditation to visualize, to desire, to expect, to imagine the realities that you want — the times that you use your beliefs and your attitudes, along with the thoughts and feelings and indeed with the choices and decisions that you make in order to create your reality — those times can be more powerful and more successful by being aware of and in touch with this energy that is the Goddess.

"Further, one of the most important keys to longevity is giving birth not to children, but to ideas, to new concepts. The ability to conceive, which is the Goddess energy, adds length to your life."

You see, the more imagination you can muster and the more you are able to image the reality you want, the more you will create that reality. The more imagination you can muster, the more you will have a will that will bring that reality into manifestation. Therefore, it becomes easier to create your own reality via programming when you are in touch with, indeed embraced by, this energy that is the Goddess.

Also, the more imagination you have, the stronger is your Dream — the Dream with a capital "D", the Dream of the future, and the Dream of the world — and the more capable you are of determining the future and of changing the course of history into the positive destiny that you desire. The more you desire, the greater is your experience, and the more powerful is the reality you create.

Secondly, by being embraced by this energy — by opening your heart and your mind to this lovingness that is the Goddess — you strengthen your motivation. You see, your deepest motivations, your purpose — your focus, as we refer to it — lie at the bottom of the pool of feelings. In order to fully understand, appreciate and utilize your reason for being, you must be willing to feel, and not only feel, but feel deeply. You must be willing to dive into the very depths of your emotions in order to grasp and then to use your purpose, your focus, your motivation, your reason for being.

Thirdly, by being aware of and then allowing this Goddess energy to create with you — by allowing the Goddess to co-create a reality with you — you produce a much healthier reality for yourself. For indeed, on a quite physical level, most are aware that illness is due mainly to denied or stuffed emotion. As you open to your ability to imagine and then to feel, you can cleanse these stuffed or denied emotions. You can free yourself, liberate yourself, from their constraint — liberate yourself from the disenfranchisement, the disorientation, the disorder and failure that their denial has produced.

Thus, by working with the Goddess energy, you are also adding to your physical health — and, quite clearly, to your emotional health, and thus the intellectual health of your whole beingness is upgraded. The intuitive health and well-being can only be benefited.

Further, one of the most important keys to longevity is giving birth not to children, but to ideas, to new concepts. The ability to conceive, which is the Goddess energy, adds length to your life. All those who live to be over 100 or more, all of them have some sense, some touch with the energy of giving birth to ideas, of giving birth to concepts. Those who live to that age have a sense, a glimpse at least, of the Goddess.

Additionally, the Goddess energy empowers you to manifest the reality that you really want. It empowers you to become a bigger piece of God/Goddess/All That Is. A key to your spirituality in this time of the '80s and '90s — the key to that which is called the New Age, and more appropriately should be called the New Spirituality — is your willingness to cross the Bridge of Belief. The key to traditional spirituality, as represented by world religions, is your willingness to take a leap of faith. The New Spirituality is based upon your willing-ness to cross the Bridge of Belief. It does not require blind faith. It requires a partnership of belief with God, with Goddess, with All That Is. The feminine energy, the energy of the Goddess, provides that Bridge of Be-lief across which you must pass to fully engage and realize your spirituality. A practical importance? Most definitely!

An additional benefit: You have heard that there is a power that lies within you. Traditional religion, tradi-tional psychology and philosophy all tell you that there is a power within. Alternative religions, alternative spir-itualities, and alternative psychologies and philosophies as well finally agree with the traditions and say that there is a power within.

Many are ready to tell you where that power lies, but very few are willing to let you get in touch with it, to tell you how to get hold of that power to do anything with it. From the misfit to the mystic, they are willing to tell you that you should be in touch with that power, but often they are unwilling to tell you how.

Getting in touch with the feminine energy by getting in touch with the Goddess, by getting in touch with that part of you that is a part of God/Goddess/All That Is, is the key. Through the harmony and ultimately the balance of that feminine energy, of that Goddess energy, you will unlock the Vortex of Power that lies within.

Lazaris: Because each person must define and then discover the Goddess for themselves, each person can engender for themselves any number of obstacles that will stand in their path of such discovery. Since the Goddess energy is such an integral part of the new spiritual growth that is emerging in your world, any obstacle that stands in the way of your spirituality can become an obstacle that stands in the way of your discovery of the Goddess energy. As many obstacles as there could be, however, we will suggest four that are the major obstacles that will probably stand in your way. If you will release each of these, we would suggest you will more likely discover that co-creating, powerful energy that is the Goddess.

Q: What are the major obstacles to working with the Goddess, and how might we deal with them?

The first obstacle is male chauvinism. When we speak of male chauvinism, we do not limit it simply to men, but rather suggest that in your world, due to the consensus reality and the way that you have been brought up — due to the parental influences, the influences of school and of church, the influences of your psychology and your medicine, the influences of peers, and even the influence of your metaphysics — you have been left in a position of being male chauvinists, women as well as men.

Male chauvinism in its simplest definition is the devaluing and disenfranchising of women simply because of their gender, and the stereotypic "less-thans" that are attached to being female. Men clearly are male chauvinists and are brought up in this capacity, and women as well are brought up to believe that by their gender they automatically are "less than." This chauvinism, evidenced in both men and women, must be broken, at least fractured or fragmented, before you will allow yourself to glimpse the Goddess energy.

The second major obstacle can be stated as simply as the first: It has to do with believing that the Goddess energy is female rather than feminine — with thinking that it has to do with being female only, rather than thinking it has to do with being human.

There will be those who will want to see the energy of the Goddess as being gendered — female — and will then resort to a reverse chauvinism of thinking that all that is female, and all that is Goddess, is somehow better than all that is male, and all that is God. They are not recognizing that the Goddess energy is a feminine *energy* and therefore without gender, an energy that is available to both women and men and is indeed ultimately, essentially, available to all who are human in their search for their spirit, for their soul, for their relationship with God/Goddess/All That Is.

"The immensity of the power that is the Goddess frightens people so much that they want to deny it."

The third obstacle comes from the consensus reality which places an inordinate value on doing and upon dynamic demonstration of what can be done, rather than on the subtle beauty and awe of being. In your world you make the mistake of assuming that anything that involves the five senses is somehow more valuable than those things that don't. If you can see it, touch it, taste it, smell it, and hear it, somehow it is more meaningful, more valuable, more worthy than if it exists outside of those five senses. You make the mistake of assuming that what you see is real.

Rather, it is the *feeling* that the sight produces that is real. You make the mistake of assuming that what you hear and what you touch and what you taste is somehow more real than the feeling that those sights, those touchings, those tastings produce. We would suggest that indeed your senses are but doorways to the reality, that the senses record illusion that engenders emotion that is real.

The state of doing is indeed important in your reality, but the state of being that lies beneath it, that lies to the left of it and the right of it, that lies ahead of it (though not recordable by your five senses) is equally as important. The subtlety and beauty and the awe of being provides the framework, the space, the ability, and the context for all that you do, all that you dynamically demonstrate in the illusion of your physicality. When you can realize this equity between doing and being, you can begin to glimpse the Goddess through the lens of being.

The final obstacle that we will suggest is that there is a tremendous fear of the immense power that is this feminine energy, that is this Goddess energy. Throughout the history of humankind there have been many religions from one time of reality to another. The ones of modern times worship a male God energy. However, we would suggest that in many Eastern philosophies still and throughout the world at large totally, there have been just as many civilizations that have worshipped the Goddess energy.

However, because of the immense power of the Goddess energy, She never feels the need to defend Herself. Throughout the history of humankind there have never been those who have gone to war to defend their Goddess. There have never been those who have killed the innocents or the "unsaved" in the name of their Goddess. There have never been those who have had to burn people and to destroy people who spoke out against their Goddess. The immensity of the power that is the Goddess frightens people so much that they want to deny it. They want to close themselves off from it. They want to pretend that it simply doesn't exist. As people, women and men, begin to glimpse the Goddess, they will again begin to understand the power.

For the Goddess energy is the initiating energy of creation. In order to create, you must first have an ability to create. In order to be powerful, you first must have an ability to be powerful, an ability to act. In order to fill a space, you must first create the space. These initiating energies are all energies of the Goddess. The ability to act which leads to power, the ability to create which leads to dynamic creation, and the creating of the space are all Goddess energies which have to come before the dynamic demonstration of manifestation.

Feminine energy initiates masculine energy. Feminine energy is so immense in its power that it does not demand recognition for this initiation, but is more than willing to allow the male energy to take credit, to be the victor, to play "king of the mountain," while the Goddess energy will be the mountain. Because of this immense power, people are afraid of this energy, and therefore shut down to it.

The way to work with these blockages is first of all to recognize them within you, to see your level of chauvinism and the level to which you, the male or the female, think the Goddess is only another form of woman. Recognize how much you value the information your senses provide you as being real, as opposed to the sensations and the emotions and the imageries that those senses engender, which you consider fantasies. Recognize your own fear of that power of life or death that the first female — mother — and then seemingly all females and eventually the Goddess seem to hold over you.

"You see, with the Goddess energy it is not necessary to march or carry placards or banners to defend Her, for Her power is immense. All you have to do is open your heart and imagine Her, and She's there."

As you can recognize these particular obstacles within you, so you can acknowledge their presence. Then it becomes important to forgive yourself, forgive yourself for each of these maladies, and then to change — to unilaterally change: Stop your chauvinism, male or female. Recognize and own that the Goddess is a feminine energy, available equally to either gender. Understand that your reality is an illusion, and what is real is the imaginings, the feelings, the conjurings of conception and perception that lie in the state of being, engulfing your illusion.

Finally, change your fear into a willingness to embrace this most wondrous and beautiful power. You do not need to create it. Rather, co-create with it. In fact, many may wonder how they might work with this Goddess energy to help it emerge, to bring it forth more into the world. Rather than getting on soap boxes, rather than going out there and trying to convince others, reach inside yourself, find your particular obstacles (these four that we have outlined or any others that come to you). Recognize them, acknowledge them, forgive yourself and change them. Open your arms and willingly, joyously, lovingly embrace this energy that is the Goddess within yourself. As you do this, lighting your own light, letting your own beacon shine, this will then inspire others who will inspire others who will inspire others.

Thus the Goddess energy will emerge, reemerge, emerge and reemerge again. You see, with the Goddess energy it is not necessary to march or to carry placards or banners to defend Her, for Her power is immense. All you have to do is open your heart and imagine Her, and She's there.

Lazaris: The very asking of the question speaks often to the limitation that people assume that the Goddess is meant just for women. They assume that men have had for all these centuries their God, with which they've pummeled the world and all societies that did not agree with them. They assume that now it is time for women to have their God who will come forth and perhaps (in the male projection) pummel men. No. The Goddess is not a female. Though she will appear to most of you in the female form, she is feminine. Within

Q: How can men work with the Goddess energy?

each man and woman there is the hidden woman that is their personal aspect of the Goddess.

Carl Jung spoke and suggested that men had a hidden woman, and that women had a hidden man, and we would suggest, with all due respect, that Carl Jung was correct only partially — that the fullest truth is that within each man there are a male and a female that lie mostly undiscovered. Within each woman there are similarly a male and a female that lie largely dormant. It is erroneously assumed that because a person has a male gender he understands what is it is to be a man, and that because a person has a female gender she understands what it is to be a woman.

That you are a man means that you have chosen to learn particularly of maleness and temper it with femaleness to become whole. That you are a woman means that you came into this incarnation to develop particularly your female energy and to temper it with your maleness to become whole.

Therefore, how can men work with the Goddess energy? In the same way as women can: to open their minds, to open their hearts, to be willing, first of all, to accept the very concept that such an energy exists and then to begin a journey, a journey that is often called spirituality, a journey home to discover it within you and without you.

Lazaris: We suggest there are any one of four (and optimally all four) of the following qualities: The first of these is love. We suggest that what would be important in becoming the maximum of who you are, and in having that connection with God/Goddess/ All That Is, is that you really learn as best you can the *skill* and the *ability* of loving — that you learn the particulars and the specifics of what to *do* to be a loving person to yourself and then to others — and what to *be* to be a loving person to yourself and then to others.

Q: What qualities are best to develop if one wants to evolve and become more of the God/Goddess/All That Is that is within us?

It is very important, in the doingness of love, to really understand that there are specific things to do. It's not just something that comes mystically, automatically, spontaneously. Giving is a very important part. Giving and responding, or being responsible. Respect is a tremendously important action/function to do. Knowing is the fourth. Then, in that sense, being humble enough to be intimate and courageous enough to be committed are the fifth and sixth. And finally, the seventh is to care, to honestly care, to be living in a reality where more and more you're working with that function of caring.

However, you do not just do those things for the sake of doing them. Rather, do those things for the very specifics of creating a certain state of awareness. Create, for example, security. Create also pleasure. Create a sense of vulnerability and truth. Create a sense of trust. Work so as to reduce the fear of loss, which is the grandest fear when love comes about. Open up to the intimacy and the caring so as to produce that state of *feeling* the intimacy and caring. And finally, create a state of knowing, where indeed you feel as though the person knows you and you know the other person.

Therefore, give not just for the sake of giving, but give to produce security, pleasure, etc. Respect a person not just for the sake of respecting, but so as to produce trust, intimacy and knowing. Sense that feeling of caring to produce vulnerability and reduce the fear of loss. Do these seven things — giving, responding, respecting, knowing, being intimate, being committed, and knowing — in order to produce these seven states: security, pleasure, vulnerability, trust, reduced fear of loss, caring and intimacy, and knowing.

The second major area to work with is the Valuing Self. Be aware and be alert to Self-Awareness. So often people look at this field in terms of "Self-awareness is the final achievement," as if it were the highest level. No, we would suggest, it is one of the first levels. To be aware of yourself, to be aware that you have impact is self-awareness. You are real. You are here. You are interacting in the world — illusion albeit — but from your point of view it's real, and therefore work with self-awareness and with your self-worth, which is knowing that you have a spiritual nature and are appreciating that spiritual nature.

Work with your self-esteem. Self-esteem is the earned love, the love that you earn not through your "good works" and through the "approval of others," but rather the esteem you earn through your honesty, through your integrity, through the responsibility and the trust that you develop.

Then, of course, self-love is part of the Valuing Self, and in that sense that is the love that you are given. It's not earned. You don't earn love, in that way. You give it to yourself.

Then there is self-confidence, your capacity to cope, to deal with the reality that you have created.

Develop self-respect, which is honoring your emotions — honoring the fact that you are an emotional being, and honoring what those emotions are.

The synergistic culmination of these values is mystically called Self-Realization. The thumbnail explanation of Self-Realization is "impact that you direct." In that sense, "Not only do I have impact, but I have the power and the dominion to direct that impact. I can have the impact I want, consciously."

Beyond the Valuing Self, the third thing to deal with is Excellence. We suggest here that you learn to function with Excellence, but not in the school sense of your childhood where you had to get straight A's or you got in trouble. Rather, work with Excellence in the sense of working with a desire and with the clarity of that desire, working both with a sense of a vision, the vision of the future, and with the impeccability of the present.

Work with elegance. We use that term not in the "fashion" sense, but in the scientific sense of expending the least amount of energy for the maximum amount of return. Develop that sense of elegance. Work with the joy of growing and with the courage of discernment. The courage, yes, to discern. People run from judgment. They don't want to be judgmental, and therefore they also abandon discernment because, in that sense, it takes courage to discern.

Open to the wisdom and understanding and ultimately to that sense which we call the Excellence of what life is. Work with that. Function that way. Know that more and more of your life is a result of the desire, the clarity, the elegance and the excellence of who you are and who you can be.

Finally, the fourth way that individually or collectively you can work toward being more of God/Goddess/All That Is is to establish a relationship with your Higher Self — first of all by accepting that there is a higher "you". There is a "you" that is beyond that which you know that is watching over you, a "you" that is a part of you, that is guiding you, if you will allow it to guide you. There is a Higher Consciousness that is within you that is not just out there beyond your reach and "someday hopefully ..."

Indeed there are ways to make contact with your Higher Self, and indeed that's a lot of what we teach, a lot of what we do in the workshops and in the seminars. A lot of what we do with people when we talk to them individually is open them up to that sense of their Higher Self so they are able to know it, not just abstractly and theoretically, but to experience that sense of it.

Therefore, work with any one of these four — whichever one feels right. "Ah, I don't know about Higher Self stuff, that seems ..." OK, fine, then. Work with one of the others, or maybe two of the others — or if you're really ambitious, maybe three. Once you've done that, you can perhaps add the fourth component. That's how you bring yourself closer to God/Goddess/All That Is. Those are the qualities and the aspects that you're looking for to make that evolutionary process of becoming more of who you are and who you can be.

Brian Enright/Lisa Michelle Guest, **Los Angeles &**
Orange County Resources, *Los Angeles*

With love and peace ...

Lazaris

Health & Disease

The Nature of Health — Alzheimer's Disease — Multiple Allergies
Addictions — The Immune System — AIDS: A Compassionate Exploration

The Nature of Health

Q: How can
we increase
our own heal-
ing abilities so
that we will
have more
vitality to ac-
complish what
we want?

Lazaris: All right ... Well, there are many, many different natural approaches, many different regimes, and a problem can arise when people try to
find out which one is objectively the right one, the best
one, which one is guaranteed more than any other,
which one is guaranteed to make them well. Each of the
many regimes can work very powerfully and very
beautifully for different people. Each person must find
their own regimen, their own approach that's going to
work for them. They can receive help, but they must
decide for themselves.

What is universal, however, is the nature of what
good health is. So often in the attempts to find healing
methods and to work with healing approaches, people
will, in a sense, jump the gun. They'll get a false start in
their race against time and space by not bothering to
stop and say, "All right, what is good health, first of
all?" They're all running around trying to find healing
or health. Many are in a mad dash trying to get as
much of it as possible. But very few have ever stopped
to say, "What is it really? What is good health? What is
the nature of health?"

Briefly, health comprises several components. The
first step to increase your own healing abilities is to
start defining for yourself what it is to be healthy, what
it means to you.

Health involves a certain aliveness, certainly so, but
first it involves a certain searching, a searching for the
reason for living, the reason for life. It is a searching for
the purpose of life, as some would want to call it. We

prefer the word focus. As well as searching, it requires a seeking, a seeking of power, a seeking of what we call the four powers — the power of freedom, the power of action, the power of giving, and the power of joy.

Being a healthy person is not just a physiological concern. It is that part of each of you that is seeking those powers — not to have power over, but to have the ability to act and to be free, the ability to be filled with action, the ability to be in that place of giving and in that place of being filled with joy.

It is also looking and finding what we call the elegance of life, where you expend the least amount of energy for the maximum amount of return. It also involves the elegance of spirituality.

Thus, it is a searching, and it is knowing your focus (purpose). It is seeking and finding of the four powers of life. It is an elegance in life — both physically and spiritually.

Finally, good health is built on aliveness. Some people who are physically alive have very little aliveness. Others, however, who may be physically incapacitated in some way may be filled with aliveness. Aliveness is measured by levels of trust, love, expectancy, and enthusiasm.

People need to look to themselves to develop this sense of: "I'm going to be searching and knowing the basic essentials of my life — where I'm going and why I'm here. I'm going to be seeking and finding my power. I'm going to be doing so with an elegance, with a grace, with a dignity, with a certain aplomb. Also, I'm going to be doing it with aliveness, filled with a vibrancy of love, filled with a vibrancy of trust, filled with a vibrancy of enthusiasm and expectation."

As people will do that, that will be the foundation upon which they can choose a regimen of health that

"You see, responsibility scares you. You live under this myth that somehow if you don't want to be responsible for your reality, you don't have to be."

can work — really work — for them. Whether it's naturopathic or homeopathic or acupunctural or whatever, this foundation of good health is important. Even following traditional means of medicine, the allopathic methods, can be so much more effective if people will establish this foundation of searching, seeking, elegance and aliveness — this foundation of what good health is.

If people will start with these bases, then they can begin their race against time and space to find the particular avenues, the particular angles, of healing that work best for them. Then whatever regimen they choose will work more productively and constructively.

*Jim Faubel, **Transformation Times**, Beaver Creek, Oregon*

Q: Some of the metaphysical community have stated that 15% of all physical illness is karmic and that the rest of the 85% of the illnesses manifested are due to mental or emotional causes. Would you comment on that?

Lazaris: Well, we love that. Fifteen percent, yes? ... {laughter} ... Now who is the statistician that figured that out? ... {laughter} ... Recording all illnesses ... there must be better things to do in your world than that! ... {laughter} ...

We suggest that 100% of illness is emotionally induced. It's no less devastating. We're not saying everybody's a hypochondriac. We didn't say that at all. Every disease has its emotional origin, even if it's a past lifetime emotional origin that you are *choosing* in this lifetime to deal with (not that you have to, not that anybody's twisting your arm or making you). There is an emotional causation in this lifetime that is causing you to reach into that past and drag that "other-life" influence here. One hundred percent of all illness is emotionally induced.

Added to that are the beliefs, the attitudes, the thoughts and feelings, the choices and decisions about illness. If you believe that a contagious disease is contagious, then it will be. If the consensus reality says it's contagious, then it's going to be more difficult to break the belief. If a disease is contagious and you come in contact with that person, will you get the disease? It depends on whether you choose to create it. Even contact contagiousness is emotionally induced.

"You tend to lodge your hurts in your spine. Any kind of back difficulty has an origin in hurt."

Now we're not going to talk about all the emotional inducements, but we will say this. Anger is the biggest one. Anger and hurt are the biggest emotional inducements of illness. Simply said, cancer is anger, as we've suggested many times — anger that you feel is hopeless and beyond repair. In the general sense, all back difficulty, no matter how physiologically induced, has its seed in pain — emotional pain — hurt.

You see, responsibility scares you. You live under this myth that somehow if you don't want to be responsible for your reality you don't have to be. Therefore, you stuff your feelings — except there's nowhere to stuff them, right? So you stuff your anger in various organs of the body, in various parts of the body, right on down to the bone. It often depends on what kind of anger it is as to where you stuff it. The various organs of the body speak to different components.

Hurt you tend to stuff in your spinal column. "Here's this lovely little column. It's pretty much hollow. Stuff it like a Christmas stocking." … {laughter} … You tend to lodge your hurts in your spine. Any kind of back difficulty has an origin in hurt. Cancers have an origin in anger. Bolemia and various forms of other food disorders such as anorexia have a tremendous amount to do with self-hatred. "I hate myself. I don't deserve to be nurtured. I don't deserve to receive love. And therefore I won't eat. Or if I do I'll throw it up, because I hate myself so much that I don't deserve any nurturing at all. Not even food do I deserve."

With various other diseases, depending on what they are, you can find an emotional origin that is the valid emotional origin — not just any emotional origin. Mainly look to anger, and mainly look to hurt, and then to self-hatred and the refusal to love. Those are the biggies. Those are the biggies.

Though we state these things simply, they do not work simply. Seldom do emotional inducements work singularly. They work in complexes and in intricate matrices with each other. Therefore, that you are angry does not mean you are destined to get cancer. Nor does it mean that if you are hurt it is only a matter of time before your back "gives out." It would also be inappropriate to say, "If I don't believe something is contagious, then it isn't. It's as simple as that." Life need not be difficult, but it is both intimate and intricate. Life and health should not be reduced to "one-liners."

So 100% of illness is caused emotionally. Therefore, if you will be responsible, you can eliminate a lot of illness. But if you do have an illness, don't blackmail yourself into thinking you're bad and wrong.

"Life and health should not be reduced to 'one-liners.'"

Illness is like a smoke alarm. It's warning you. It's telling you: Here's a problem. Sometimes the smoke alarm goes off, and it's too late, and the house burns down. Eh, you can always get another house. Sometimes it goes off soon enough that you can make the corrections. Sometimes you can create miracles and make the corrections even when it's too late. Don't blackmail yourself by being ashamed of your illness. Listen to the alarm and respond. Responsibly respond.

All illness is emotionally induced. When you say that, people think it's hypocondria, it's psychological, it's not real. No, it's real. It's real. It'll show up on every x-ray. It'll show up on every test. It'll play itself out, and it is very real. In the illusion, it is very real. So don't discount a disease. "Oh, that's just your emotions."

There is nothing else. There are just your emotions. They are everything in your life.

Anonymous Question, Atlanta Evening with Lazaris, 1987

Alzheimer's Disease

azaris: Alzheimer's Disease, as you know, is a fairly new disease. It affects people usually after the age of 40. You were hoping we'd say 80, yes? ... {laughter} ... Anytime after 40 you're more susceptible to Alzheimer's than you are prior to 40, although there will be a time when some 20-year-olds will contract Alzheimer's Disease.

Q: Alzheimer's Disease. Would you please speak about it?

The origin of all disease and illness is emotional, but physiology can have impact. Physiology alone cannot cause illness, but it can work as a strong and significant ally. It creates hurdles that often need to be overcome. It's important to understand and cooperate with the physical messages of illness.

Physiologically, it has to do with your brain, and contamination of the brain. A lot of it has to do with metal contamination such as aluminum contamination of the brain. Therefore, we do not encourage you to use those little spray mouth fresheners because they have aluminum in them, and you don't know that it's not going up into your brain.

We'll scare you a little more: We'd stay away from cake mixes, because they also have aluminum in them. Therefore, if your friends must eat cake — let them eat cake — bake it yourself. ... {laughter} ... Stay away from the packaged mixes if you can, because they also have aluminum. Stay away from aluminum that leaches into the body.

After a period of time aluminum builds up and lodges in the brain and produces, physiologically, a propensity toward Alzheimer's Disease. That's why it doesn't affect people under 40 — yet — because it takes time for the contamination to build up, just as mercury or lead poisoning takes time to build up in the body. This is one of the major physiological origins of Alzheimer's Disease.

They are going to discover, by the way, that aluminum is not the only basis of Alzheimer's. Alzheimer's also will relate to the function of the pituitary and the function of the pineal gland, most specifically the pineal gland and certain secretions that come from the pineal gland that, when wrongly put forth, can cause a haywire activity in the brain and thus produce Alzheimer's Disease.

It's a very, very sad illness. It is sad for the person involved, because they have spells of lucidity and spells where they don't know what's going on. They don't know where they are. They don't know who they are. They don't know who the people in the house with them are. They live together with someone for 40 or 50 years, and ... "Who is that person? I don't know who that is." It's very frightening for the person, and it's very frightening and very sad for the people who have to live with and deal with the afflicted person.

To discover the emotional origin, we would first ask: Why are they shutting down? Why do they want to close their minds to the world in which they live? It may be anger, it may be hurt, it may be disillusionment, it may be some sort of pain, it may be a hopelessness, a helplessness — any number of reasons. Look first to that. If that doesn't make sense to you, then start looking at other ways they might have shut down, other ways in which they want to shut their brain off. Perhaps it's a sense of impotence that says, "I have no outlet for all that goes on in my mind."

The way to avoid Alzheimer's? Stay away from aluminum? You can't really do that. More effectively, stay creative. Stay creative. Always have something creative to do. And always have productive work, work, work. You see, you've got a belief about work that it is hard and what you want to avoid. We would suggest no. Work is essential — productive work, not just work for the sake of working. Productive work and creativity. Always be creative. No matter how public or private your creativity is, be creative. If you want to be a writer, write. If you want to be a painter, paint. It doesn't matter if anybody likes it, if anybody buys it. Create. When you're 92, create. Create and work. Work. Absolutely work.

"Always work. Always create. You'll stay healthier and live longer, absolutely."

The oldest groups of people on your planet live in Georgia (Russia) and in places in South America and India. What they have in common with each other is that they work all their lives. They are 120 years old, and they're out in the fields working. They work, and they create. They don't have a lot of means, but they create in their mind. They have active imaginations, which they value and on which they place importance. They are creating, all the time creating. You look at some of the people that live the longest in your world. They are creating. When you stop creating and you stop working, that's when you start dying, and that's when you're apt to shut down.

So, you see, this brain of yours is working. It is creating. Researchers used to think your brain was just a passive receiver. They don't think that anymore. They know, your scientists, something we have suggested all along: Your brain is actively thinking whether you are or not.

When you stop thinking and the brain keeps thinking, that creates pressure, that creates crisis. One of the ways you handle that crisis is to shut your brain off. Alzheimer's is one way to do that.

Those that say, "I want to get rich so I don't have to work anymore," are, in a certain way, signing their own death warrants early. You look at anybody who's tremendously weathly and old, and they're working, always working. Some say, "Look at so-and-so. He must be greedy. He's got all the money he needs. Why is he still working?" We say, "Because he wants to stay alive to enjoy the money that he's created!" Be working, creative. Always work. Always create. You'll stay healthy and live longer, absolutely. Two of the secrets to longevity there, and a response to Alzheimer's.

Anonymous Question, Atlanta Evening with Lazaris, 1987

Multiple Allergies

Q: There's a recent finding that some multiply allergic people are sensitive to electricity and electrical equipment.

Lazaris: In most cases, these people are allergic to the 20th Century. Their delicate "body electric" has difficulty integrating with the highly technological world in which you now live.

You see, each cell in your body is like a charged battery. When you are healthy, those "batteries" are all charged and running smoothly. When those battery-like cells have lost their charge, or are running irregularly, you call it illness. These multiply allergic people are losing their charge or running irregularly.

Their bodies are not in full alignment with the electromagnetic field they are living in. They are allergic to the 20th Century.

The overall ambience was once much more harmonious. Such allergies were unusual or nonexistent 50 to 100 years ago because there was little electricity. Radio waves, microwave transmissions, cable TV, and other inventions of electro-technology have effect — have impact — on the resonance of the Earth's ambient electrical pattern.

Well, you cannot turn off technology, and the multiply allergic person cannot just "pass" on this lifetime. There are solutions.

The brain/mind, for example, generates sufficient electrical energy that it can create its own field of energy to counter the dissonance. Even though this is a high-tech problem, metaphysical principles of processing and programming still work. In fact, they work wonderfully well on these kinds of problems.

People can also use quartz crystals placed on electrical equipment to mitigate the potentially damaging influence. A simple natural quartz crystal on your personal computer can work wonders. Another on your television can produce a subtle, but effective, result.

Some may find that wearing a copper coil — a bracelet perhaps — can help create an electronic balance. A few years ago, copper bracelets were quite popular. However, the copper coil should not form a complete circle. The ends should come close to each other, but should not meet.

There are a number of potential answers for the multiply allergic. The key is to figure out why emotionally they are having this allergic response to the 20th Century. The answers to this question will allow remedies

to work or not work. Illness begins on the emotional
level — always.

*Marilyn Ferguson, **Brain/Mind Bulletin**, October, 1987, 3rd issue.*

Addictions

Q: What messages are people giving themselves with addictions?

Lazaris: Addictions offer many messages. Each person who chooses to be addicted, and then creates logical, tangible explanations and realities to generate those addictions, does so for different reasons. Some of the more common messages are self-destructive; however, some addictions are actually survival mechanisms that have outlived their usefulness.

The main message of an addiction is: "I want to hide. I do not believe I can handle my world. I am out of control. I must hide." Most often the message is self-destructive and based on a severe lack of love. These people feel that they cannot and do not love "good enough," and therefore they are terrified of being found out, so they hide. If they fail at loving, they can blame their addiction, not themselves. They are safe, at least for a little while. Often these addictions begin when the person really cannot cope, really does not have the capacity to know they do indeed love "good enough." Thus, the addiction, we would suggest, begins as a survival method, perhaps even an inventive survival mechanism, which has outlived its usefulness.

Often addictions begin in your teen or young adult years when the pragmatic truth is that you have not learned, nor developed, methods of loving. You have not learned how to love, nor have you developed methods of loving or assessing your ability to love. In a panic, you must suddenly be an adult, handling adult responsibilities and situations.

The disbelief in themselves and their lack of adequate tools and feedback mechanisms leave them unable to cope — really unable to cope — with their reality. They hide in order to survive — and literally they must, and feel they must, hide in order to survive.

Now, however, they can be an adult. They have method and feedback. If they will come out of their hiding places, they can learn and experience. They can cope. They don't have to hide any more.

The second message: "I do not deserve to be happy and free." Often, because the inventive survival mechanism has gone sour, they feel undeserving of happiness and freedom. After all, they feel, if they deserved it, they would have it. It is circular reasoning, we know, but it is often what happens to people with their addictions. Due to the addiction, they feel tremendous shame and tremendous despair. Maybe now they can cope with and face the world with love, but alas, now they cannot cope with the shame and the despair. They feel that they do not deserve to be loved, that they do not deserve to be happy, that they do not deserve to be free.

The third message: "I am weak." These people feel and think that their addiction is a legitimate crutch. They feel they cannot function without whatever it is they are addicted to. When people give power away they can easily become addicted to that to which they give their power. Whether you give your power away to a guru or to a powder, to a liquid or to a weed, the very giving away of the power itself becomes an addictive behavior, something that people feel they cannot live without. They feel they somehow must continue to give away that power even when they know verbally, mentally, that it's not to their advantage.

The fourth message: "I'm a product of my society. This is what they have done to me." In other words, it is a message of blame. It is initially, perhaps, a way of releasing anger. When stuffed, filled to the brim, and overflowing with resentments and angers, it may seem the only viable method of release. Certain individuals turn to addictive behaviors of self-destructiveness — and cut off their own nose, as it were — to try to get the message across that "I'm hurting. I'm in pain. I'm angry." However, this system of release ultimately backfires and turns into a self-destructiveness that is addiction. The initial blame is of "them." The subsequent blame is of the addicted person.

These are four — not all — but four of the messages that addictions bring. Each could have begun as a legitimate, though short-sighted, response to a real concern. Each could have been helpful in a limited way in finding a temporary solution to a very legitimate problem. However, a technique becomes addictive when it outlives its usefulness. Systems also can become addictive as well.

Q: How does one determine if something is an addiction or not? What are the criteria?

Lazaris: We would at this point suggest four criteria of evaluation. The first: The basic way to evaluate behavior and to assess its real or potential addictiveness is to check your motivation and your feedback. Define the behavior in question, and then ask yourself several questions:

Am I doing this to become more of who I am?

HEALTH & DISEASE 125

Is the behavior bringing me closer to who I can potentially be?

Am I hiding? Am I avoiding my future and who I am becoming?

Once you have asked these questions, it becomes then important to evaluate your feedback. It is easy to lie to yourself, but your reality often will expose the lie. You may tell yourself that you are becoming more of who you are and closer to your future, but what is factually true in your reality? What is your reality feeding back to you? How much happier are you? How much more successful are you? What is really happening in your world?

Also, what do your friends think and say about how well you're doing? What? You have no friends!? It well could be an addiction ...

The second checkpoint is to assess your circle of intimates and friends. If there is a sudden change in that circle that is not consciously created and specifically programmed, then it could be an early warning signal that indeed you are either dangerously close to, or deeply involved in, an addictive behavior.

Thirdly, ask yourself: Are you loving yourself more? This does not mean: Are you approving of or praising yourself more? Many people involved in the height of their addiction will be preoccupied with approvals and praises. What it does mean is: Are you really loving yourself more? Are you giving and responding and respecting yourself more than you were before? Are you knowing yourself more and better than ever before? Are you indeed more intimate, more committed and more caring about yourself?

Are all of these activities leading to a more secure, more pleasurable reality where you feel a greater sense of vulnerability and trust of yourself? Are your fears of losing in your reality being substantially reduced? Are you feeling more intimacy and caring in your life as a whole? And are you honestly — and we mean honestly — coming to know yourself more? If the answer to these questions is that you are indeed engaging in these activities, and you are producing these results, we would suggest here that you are probably not involved in an addictive behavior.

Fourthly: If you are achieving positive results while using this potentially addictive behavior, are you also achieving the same or better results without that behavior? If you are not, it could well be an addiction.

It is of interest to note, for example, that one of the earlier experimenters with LSD was Aldous Huxley. It is reported in his writings, and in the writings of those who wrote about him, that in his entire life of many, many years of experimenting with LSD, his actual consumption of the drug — in his entire life — was far less than what most people today consume in one session.

There was an example of someone using a drug to explore, to pioneer new states of awareness, not to become addicted to it. Subsequently, others, using the rationale of such exploration, indeed indulged and overindulged to the point of becoming very addicted and ultimately burning out.

You have to evaluate it for yourself. You have to come to your own truth as to this potential. Are you using the drug to heighten your experience and then to discover it on your own, or are you using the drug to create the experience only?

These are criteria of evaluation; they are not absolute rules. Each person, in considering and evaluating their own potential and real addictions, needs to use these criteria fluidly.

Lazaris: The basis for any change is first of all to recognize the problem and then to acknowledge it. Once it has been so acknowledged, you are in a position where you can honestly forgive yourself. And after forgiveness comes change. These four criteria are the four bases, the four movements of energy, that are required to produce any kind of change, whether you do that spiritually or via the consensus reality.

Q: How do you deal with addictions spiritually rather than using the traditional consensus reality methods?

Often, however, the consensus reality sets forth a structure of change that begins, indeed, with recognition, but then moves into blaming others or finding excuses and rationales. It turns thirdly to blaming yourself, being self-critical and self-denying and self-punishing. You are hoping that out of this will come change. Obviously, it does not work.

If you will recognize your addiction, you must first decide what, if anything, you really want to do about it. There are certain addictions that may be imposing self-harm and have no particular impact upon anyone else in your reality. Even so, you may still decide that you don't particularly care to change or work with or alter in any way your addictive behavior. If that is your choice, then that is your choice. Make it, and don't bother trying to change your addiction. Don't put yourself through the twists and turns and paces that will lead you nowhere. If you really do not mind your addiction, and no one else is really adversely affected, you may want to go ahead and keep your addiction. That is fine. You see, we do not judge you or your addiction.

If, however, you do want to change after you make the recognition, really recognizing and owning the addiction, then we advise you acknowledge it. More than just a word, acknowledgement means you must really *own* the particular addiction. It is important to root out the cause, the initial survival mechanism if there is one, and to understand it as fully and completely as you can, and then to see how it went wrong, where it outlived its usefulness, its purposefulness, its value. Own the fact that it is your addiction.

"Do not become addicted to your method of change. Realize it is you who is causing the changing."

We have sometimes used an analogy about a grand and glorious bridge in the San Francisco area, the Golden Gate Bridge. If you rather go downtown anywhere in the world and offer to sell that bridge they might well lock you up, because you don't own it. But if indeed you could produce papers to prove that it was yours, then not only would you not be locked up, you would rather be treated in a grand and glorious style.

Therefore, you cannot get rid of what you do not own. You cannot get rid of your addiction until you own that it is, indeed, yours, and that you are the source, that you are the cause. It is your addiction. Nobody made you do it. You chose it yourself.

By this point, just when you are sure that you are the lowest scum on the Earth, forgive yourself. This forgiveness, again, is more than just a word, but it is also the word as well. It is important to really dig in and to honestly forgive yourself and to *say* so, to hear the words spoken, to see the words written: "I forgive myself. I am forgiven."

It may take several times, several attempts, several passes, to fully and honestly forgive yourself. Once you have forgiven yourself, however, the change can take place in a number of ways, in any number of forms, from a simple decision to a very elaborate support system. The methods may vary, but the common base is desire for, imagination to, and expectation of — *and expectation of* — change.

Do not become addicted to your method of change. Realize it is you who is causing the changing. Therefore, seek and find a method — whether it is a book you read, a television show you watch, a workshop you attend, an elaborate detoxification program in which you enroll — it doesn't really matter. You are the cause of the addiction. You are the cause of change. You are the cause of your freedom. Give your power to yourself rather than giving it to the addiction or to the cure of the addition.

Perhaps it becomes clear then, in looking at what the messages of addiction are, at what the criteria of evaluation are, and at what the ways of changing are, that addictions have a great deal to do with power, whether you give it away, or whether you keep it for yourself.

*Krysta Gibson, **The Seatle New Times** & **Spiritual Women's Times**, Seattle*

The Immune System

Lazaris: The metaphysical implications of the immune system are so obvious that they are often overlooked. The immune system is the defense of the body. It is the intricate network of players with unusual names like T-cells (both T-4's and T-8's), fighter cells, tighters, helper cells, and antibodies that roam the body via the blood stream in search of any alien energy from which the body needs defense. It is the system that protects you from invasion. It is the system that protects you from being a victim of "the world out there," of the unknown.

The immune system corresponds to your level of self-confidence. Self-confidence is your ability to cope with

Q: More and more we are hearing about diseases related to the immune system. What does all this mean metaphysically? What are people creating here?

the world. Confidence is composed of trust and humility entwined with hope and courage.

Trust begins with listening to the whispers of your body, your mind (intellect), your heart (feelings), and your intuition. To listen, yes. But trust is more than just listening. It is creating a synergy — a whole that is greater than the sum of the parts — of these various messages. It is not just responding to the nervous stomach or sweaty palm. It is not just listening to the rambles of logic, the flow of feelings, or the flash of insight feebly or profoundly called "knowing." It is combining all of these and mixing well to create a whole that is somehow more. That whole is trust.

Humility is the ability and the willingness to see each day as new. Even though something has always been "this way," today it could be different. Even though the boss has always been …! Today the boss could be different. Being humble is never taking a situation or a person for granted. It is a willingness to see the freshness of each moment. When you trust yourself — really trust yourself (not just saying the words) — it is easy to be humble. When you openly develop humility there is room to trust.

Hope is not the blind faith of the traditional or Fundamentalist past. Hope is a willingness to see, in the scatter of the present, the dreams, the treasures, of the future. It is an ability to sort through the actuality of today and pick out the pieces of probability and possibility for tomorrow.

"Humility is the ability and the willingness to see each day as new."

Courage is the willingness to find solutions — elegant solutions — to fears, doubts, and confusions. It is a determination to find solutions when the consensus reality says there are no more solutions left. The courageous person knows they create their own reality and acts upon that knowledge.

When trust and humility are denied, when hope and courage are broken, there is a breach of confidence — there is a breach in your ability to cope in your exterior world. The immune system reflects that breach in your ability to cope with your internal world. Globally, there has been a breach of confidence and now your world reflects that breach with a rash of immune deficiency diseases of which AIDS is only one "syndrome."

"It's time. Your world is telling you. Your body is telling you. It's time."

The immune system also corresponds to your level of defenselessness and, conversely, your level of defensiveness. If a person feels totally defenseless in their personal world or global world they are running a risk of developing a self-attaching deadly disease, an immune deficiency disease — a defense system deficiency disease — for the defenseless feel there is no hope, no help, no possible future. They feel there are no more Dreams.

The defensive person, at first glance, seems to be the total opposite from the helpless one. They do not need anyone. They can do it all themselves. That they will not take help does not mean they do not need help. They are filled with the same fears, doubts and confusions as the defenseless. They feel the same hollow and haunting pain of hopelessness — otherwise they would not need to be so defensive. They shut people out, because they do not want anyone to see the pain. That does not mean they do not feel it!

Sometimes the level of defenselessness/defensiveness is so deep that the only way out is to die. To some, it is the only hope and the only answer. The method of defense has turned against the person. The method of defense is destroying them. This is exactly what the numerous immune deficiency syndromes are doing.

The level of persistent self-pity also is reflected by the immune system. Physiologically, the immune system is the system that keeps you from being a victim of the world and of the unknown. However, if emotionally you insist/persist in being a victim or a martyr despite the alternatives — even when you "know better" — your immune system may reflect your stubbornness.

Does this mean that if you lack confidence or are either defenseless or defensive or are pitying yourself that you are doomed? NO! NO! NO! Neither does it mean that self-confidence, openness, and lack of pity guarantee safety. Each person creates and listens to the whispers differently.

So many are quick to look at the rash of immune deficiency diseases as God's punishment, as an outgrowth of the ugliness of the Human Condition, or as a hocus-pocus evilness. These immature responses are not only bogus, but are further symptoms of the denied trust and humility, of the broken hope and courage. They are another form of the breach of confidence, and the epidemic rise of defenseless/defensive reaction to a world fewer are able and willing to understand. These fear responses to real concerns only further the very self-pity that is at the core of the problem. Not only are these kinds of explanations bogus, they are damaging because they foster the problem. They fan the flames of panic.

If you want to find a solution to the attack on the human immune system, as well as a solution for the people whom you know who are dying, begin by looking at your self-confidence, your openness, and your willingness to walk away from the seduction of self-pity. Then look beyond yourself to the world which is also your creation and your responsibility.

There are many immune-balancing chemicals and diets and exercise regimes that are increasingly available. Some are wonderful; some are not.

Building your immune system, building the human immune system, begins with building a personal self-confidence. It begins with developing trust, humility, hope and courage to be fully who you are and who you can be. It begins with dropping your defenselessness or defensiveness and replacing it with the strength and power of vulnerability. It begins with walking away from the addiction of self-pity.

It's time. Your world is telling you. Your body is telling you. It's time.

Brian Enright/Lisa Michelle Guest, **Los Angeles &**
Orange County Resources, *Los Angeles*

AIDS

Louise Hay asked Lazaris if he would make an audio tape about AIDS. His response was to do more. Lazaris recorded a 90-minute tape that includes a powerfully moving meditation. He donated the time and the tape to The Hay Foundation. The Hay Foundation is the sole distributor of the tape and retains all the proceeds.

The response to this tape has been remarkable. One of the many wonderful things about this discussion is that Lazaris talks of AIDS not as a Gay disease and thus a Gay problem, but as a Human disease and Human problem that requires all of us to work together. Following is a transcription of:

"AIDS: A Compassionate Exploration."

Lazaris: Well, all right. It is a pleasure to be here talking with you. However, we want to do more than just talk with you today. We want to actually work with you. We want to work with your consciousness to help you understand this monster called AIDS. Therefore, as we are talking to you now, we are going to discuss a number of subjects and a number of matters in a very brief period of time, but know that we are also working between the words.

Contained upon this tape is a vibration, is a frequency of energy, a frequency of energy with which we can touch you, with which we can love you if you will allow yourself to be touched, if you will allow yourself to be loved, because we do not want just to talk with you. There are many who will talk, and it's wonderful when they do, but you need to open yourself, you need to let yourself be touched as well as talked to. Therefore, we want to work with your consciousness to help you understand this monster called AIDS.

Now there are many sources of information that can provide you with the valuable facts and figures that are indeed essential in the fighting of AIDS. Further, we would encourage you, grandly we would encourage you, to gather as much of this factual information as you can, both so that you understand, so that you can educate yourself, so that you can become aware of the information, become aware of the intellectual understandings, and also so that you can be aware of what the Collective Unconscious, what the Consensus Reality, what the Mass Reality out there is telling you.

Indeed it is a cliché, but education will be a main contributor in the victory — and the victory will be there. Education will be a main contributor in the victory in this battle. The ultimate contributor? Love. Of course, love.

Now because our time with you is brief, we want to rather immediately turn our attention to the metaphysical messages and meanings of AIDS. The physical messages and meanings of AIDS you can gather, and many of you already have. It is the metaphysical that we want to focus upon.

The Metaphysical Opportunity

For you see, by understanding the emotional truths of AIDS, even when some of those truths are not so very pleasant and might not be so much fun to look at, by understanding these emotional truths you can more elegantly prevent and contain the disease personally — prevent the disease personally, and for some of you, where that is no longer possible, you can hopefully allow yourselves to contain the disease personally. As you allow yourself to understand the emotional truths, you can more powerfully change the course of the future to prevent or contain the spread of AIDS to others, to prevent and contain the spread of AIDS worldwide.

Now, we are not offering a cure. No, this time together is not a medical device. It is a metaphysical opportunity. By doing more than just talking with you, indeed by touching you between the words we speak, by working with your subconscious and your unconscious mind during our discussion, and more particularly and more powerfully during the meditation, we offer an opportunity. We offer you an opportunity of power, of responsibility. We offer you an opportunity to have profound impact on your own health and the health of thousands of others. If you are willing, you can have a far-reaching impact on the health of the world, not just as it relates specifically and directly to AIDS, but as it relates to all health and all states of well-being throughout the world.

"Well, now, how can I have such impact?" you may wonder. As you're listening to our words, you may be thinking, "That sounds awfully wonderful, that sounds awfully nice, Lazaris, but how can I have such impact?" And we would answer that by telling you something that you really already know — and that is telling you that you create your own reality by either choosing to cause it, or by allowing others to cause it for you, and thus often "to you."

We want to repeat that: You do create your own reality — absolutely, absolutely. There is no fine print; there is no asterisk; there is no exception to that. You create your own reality, but you do it two ways: There are certain things in your reality that you choose to cause, those things that you are directly involved in, those things that have impact on your reality, and then there are also things in your reality that you know you did not cause. You did not overtly decide and take direct steps to make something happen.

More innocuously, for example, you are not personally responsible for the apartheid in South Africa. You are not personally responsible for the starvation in any parts of the world, etc. You did not *do* something. You did not take away the food. You did not refuse to send the food. You did not do anything choosing consciously to create that reality, but you did allow others to cause this reality for you. You either cause it by choice, or allow it by choice.

You see, you hold certain beliefs and attitudes. You make certain choices and decisions, and you have certain thoughts and feelings, and these are the raw materials that you use either to cause or allow manifestation in your reality. Each of you, through the attitudes and the beliefs that you hold, through the decisions and choices that you make, have made, and indeed will make tomorrow and the next day — each of you, based upon what you think and what you feel — is causing or allowing AIDS to be a reality in your world. Some of you are doing so quite directly by contracting it; others of you, quite indirectly, by knowing others who have contracted it.

You see, AIDS is not just a message for a few. It does not just have meaning for a limited few. AIDS is speaking to everyone on your planet. Everyone is affected in one way or another by this monster that is called AIDS. Though the virus will not infect everyone, it will have affect on everyone. The sooner you — each of you — realizes this, the sooner real progress can be made.

You allow AIDS to be a part of the consensus reality either actively, by contracting it, or passively by knowing others who have. You either choose to create it for yourself, or you allow others to create it in themselves so that you might hear the messages and learn the meanings. Either way, it is your reality, and you are creating it to learn, to understand, to hear the messages and the meanings — each of you, all of you, everyone on your planet — to learn and to understand the messages and the meanings.

Once you listen to the whispers which indeed have turned into shouts — and for many, the whispers have turned into deadly shouts — once you learn the messages, you can prevent and you can contain AIDS personally and specifically. You can then prevent and contain AIDS throughout your reality. Once you listen to the whispers and hear the messages and the shouts — once you gain the understanding and implement the understanding, then there is no reason for this to exist.

You would have no more method, no more reason, to continue to create it, and therefore you would begin, however slowly or rapidly you are willing, to un-create it. That is how you can have this impact. That is how you can put it together in such a way as to honestly say that by learning and understanding, you can change the reality for yourself personally, for those in your reality around you less personally, and for the world as a whole more impersonally. If you will own the responsibility that you create your reality by causing it or allowing it, then you can own the responsibility for un-creating it or un-allowing it.

AIDS Is Not a Gay Disease

You know, initially there were many who thought AIDS had nothing to do with them. Either because of their lifestyle, or because of their ignorance, they thought that they were somehow immune to this particular malady. They said it was a "Gay Disease." It is "God's punishment of homosexuals," they would bellow, with some sort of vague reference to Sodom and Gomorrah, not really knowing anything of what they spoke. Their rantings and their ravings not only exposed their ignorance and often their bigotry, but also slowed the progress of encountering and conquering this disease.

There were those from the Fundamentalist conservative to the very *avante garde* metaphysical, we're sorry to say, who did point fingers of blame and wanted to say that this was God's way of striking back, that this was God's way of punishing people. On the other side of it, they talked of a God who's all loving — but yet is punishing. "This is God's way of getting back at the homosexuals," they would say, even though it began as a heterosexual disease and only was carried forth in a homosexual community. They said that it was God's punishment of the unfavored.

However, they were not dealing with the fact that even within the community Lesbians are the least of those subjected to this particular malady. Are these critics, therefore, by implication, suggesting that Lesbians are perhaps God's chosen few? We would doubt very much that those who put forth such an argument would want to live with that conclusion.

No, since the initial fears and the initial panics and the initial emergence and bubblings forth of the ignorance and bigotry, you have come to realize that AIDS is not a "Gay Disease," but indeed a disease that affects everybody. AIDS is not God's punishment, nor is it cellular rebellion, nor any of the other crazy and cockamamie ideas that progress in a degenerative way to slow, to stop the potential and the possibility of overcoming this problem.

Now people, at least many people, are knowing better — not all the people, mind you — but many people are knowing better. They're realizing that this is a concern that doesn't just affect those who are sexually active — homosexual or heterosexual — or who are drug-involved or who are hemophiliacs or otherwise drug-transfusion involved. More and more people are now realizing that this affects everybody in one way or another, and indeed, as we've suggested, the sooner everybody realizes AIDS is *their* disease, *their* creation, the sooner success will be a part of everyone's reality, also.

There are many who will never ever even come close to actually contracting this virus. The disease is still theirs. AIDS still has metaphysical messages and meanings for all of you, and for your entire world.

What are these messages? Primarily there are four of them:

A Message: Defenselessness

First of all, what happens with this particular disease? What happens is that the immune system is deficient. Acquired Immune Deficiency Syndrome. It very clearly puts forth exactly what happens: A person acquires an immune deficiency. A virus takes over the body in such a way as to systematically destroy the immune system.

Now, what does the immune system do? The immune system is the system in the body that defends you from what? Disease. Viruses. Bacterial influence. The immune system defends the body against the alien environment that surrounds you. When the immune system is gone, when the immune system has been destroyed — and that's exactly what this virus does, it destroys the immune system, and then moves on — what is happening to you? You are left defenseless. You have no defense against those outside influences. You have no defense against the world that surrounds you. You have no defense. You are defenseless.

The first message of AIDS is a message of defenselessness. It is a message that you are telling yourself. "I feel defenseless in my world." Indeed people, regardless of their sexual preferences, who feel defenseless make themselves very susceptible, very susceptible to an acquired immune deficiency syndrome, because of that very defenselessness. "I am totally helpless. I am totally defenseless. I have nothing in my world. Nothing will ever help. Nothing will ever do any good. There is no solution — there is no light at the end of the tunnel. Indeed there is not even a tunnel!"

They are destroying their means of taking care of themselves. They are consciously trying to believe, and indeed are almost sometimes arrogantly and angrily trying to convince everybody around them, that there is no hope, that there is no defense for them, that they are a total victim of their world. They are totally floating free in the craziness of a world that surrounds them, bashed and battered about, at the whim of anything and everybody but themselves. People who have dedicated themselves to being victims, people who have dedicated themselves to convincing themselves and everyone around them that they are defenseless are also arguing for the limitation and may well create it through AIDS.

A Message: Defensiveness

The second message of this particular monster is that of defensiveness. Such a person says to themselves: "I am not defenseless, no, no, no. I can take care of myself. In fact, I need no help from anybody. In fact, I need nothing from anybody. In fact, nobody's going to take care of me except me, and I'm going to do it through intimidation, through manipulation, through control, through domination — through whatever I have to do. I will defend myself, and you can tell me nothing. You can teach me nothing. You have nothing to offer me, and I don't want anything from you, either."

A defensive person that you try to reach out to, to point out where they might be having problems, where things might be going wrong, where they might be misunderstanding or misinterpreting the reality, and who doesn't want to hear that, who doesn't want to see that. That person is totally defensive. They don't want to let that in at all.

When you try to talk to them of their childhood, or about their past, you hear, "No, no, no, that has nothing to do with it." They can take care of it. They don't need your advice. They don't need your help. They don't need anything. They are alone in the world, and they are going to stay that way. They are walled off in an icy exterior of defensiveness. Their immune system is similarly being given the message through this situation called AIDS.

You see, you try to learn in this physicality, and your Higher Self, whether you're in touch with it or not, tends to communicate with you to try to reach you, to try to touch you. It'll show you your defensiveness or your defenselessness first through your victimhood, through your martyrhood, through your self-pity. But if you won't listen to those messages, and, in fact, ignore those messages, and, in fact, use those messages to create a criterion for your existence, then we would suggest you present yourself in such a way as to hear the message more loudly, more loudly, more loudly, until finally the message is deafening, until finally the message kills you.

Defenselessness and defensiveness are the first two and perhaps the loudest whispers, the loudest deadly shouts, of AIDS that not only influence and affect those who actually have contracted it, but are messages to those who have to watch (either from a close space or from a far distance) the defenseless and the defensive degenerate, deteriorate, and die. Hear the whispers. Hear the message. Change the reality.

A Message: Clinging to the Past

The third message is a desperate clinging to the past. You see, some of you are very angry in your childhood. The little boy or the little girl inside of you feels that you were not treated fairly, that you were not loved properly, that somebody — whether it's mother or father or somebody in the family, somebody in the "blood"— didn't love you "good enough," didn't take care of you properly. Perhaps more aggressively, more actively, they hurt you. They reached out and damaged you in some way, and you're angry, and you are going to remain angry.

You are desperately clinging to that past because you don't want that anger to go away. You don't want that anger to be forgotten. You don't want that anger to be let go of, and therefore you hold very desperately to what we call the blood anger of the past, anger toward mother, father, siblings, or the childhood circumstance, or the constellation of family.

Whatever it is, you must decide. You must look to the part of you that clings to that past, that keeps it alive because you want to continue to blame or to point a finger or because you want to keep hold of that anger. We call it a "blood anger," because what does AIDS do? It affects the blood, and it is transmitted through blood, as well as other very precious fluids of the body most definitely, but through blood.

Therefore, it speaks to the blood anger or the family anger, the parental family anger, the blood family anger. Therefore those who hang on — those who insist that "they did it to me, and I'm going to live my life to prove that they did it to me" — make themselves susceptible. You make yourself open to the possibility of AIDS, which will be a message to you to try to tell you that this is the consequence of that clinging, that this is the consequence of holding onto that anger, that this is the result of it — a message to try to encourage you to let go, to release, to be done with it.

A Message: Desiring To Know Who Loves You

The fourth message of this dreadful condition is a desperate desire to know who loves you. One thing — and we've talked to many, many people who've contracted this disease — all of them say is, "Well, one good thing has come out of this: At least I know who loves me and who does not." Other messages: "It's heartening, at least, despite all the pain and the despair, to find out that so many people care."

We would suggest the message of AIDS is just that: Some of you are in a position where you don't think people love you, or you don't know if they do, or you're not sure if they do, and your curiosity gets so strong that it turns to desperation: "I must know who loves me! I must know who cares! And that desire is so strong that I'm willing to die to find out." If you are so desperate to find out who loves you that you're willing to die just to find the answer, indeed you will attract this energy that could manifest itself as AIDS.

The messages are quite simple therefore: Those who attract this to them, either directly or indirectly, are trying to speak to themselves of their own defenselessness or their own defensiveness. They're trying to speak to themselves about the importance of the blood anger of their past and of letting go of it. They're trying to speak to themselves in terms of "learn, learn who loves you," but don't be so desperately desirous and so desperately curious that you're willing to die for it. Those are the messages.

And what are the meanings? The meanings overlap. The fourth message is indeed the first meaning, and there are three in addition to that.

A Meaning: Learning Who Loves You

First of all, the meaning of AIDS is that it is time in your world for all of you, each of you, closely or not so closely involved in this thing called AIDS, to learn who loves you. You need to develop criteria, you need to develop methods, of learning who loves you.

A Meaning: Learning New Levels of Love

Secondly, the meaning is that it is time in your world now to learn new levels of love, to add to the existing levels, to expand from the existing levels, but to learn new levels of love. You see, this particular disease has affected the male homosexual community initially quite extensively because in that community, more than in any other, the expression of love was limited to the Second Chakra — not that all homosexuals only loved from the Second Chakra, from their genitals — no, no, no! Please do not mis-understand us here. However, there is a predominance of that orientation in that community.

Even those of you who are members of that community must admit that in your groupings and in your politic, the message was expressed very clearly: Express your love genitally. The message of AIDS is: To love *only* from the

Second Chakra, to love only from your genitals, won't work.

Look at it more closely. Even as AIDS has spread from that community to the heterosexual community, it has spread through the sexual energy — not through the promiscuity, but through the sexual energy. Therefore, in that sensing, men who sought prostitutes or who sought illicit sex of some sort and women who sought illicit sex of some sort as a way, desperately, to be clandestinely loving, have carried this disease from one group to another.

In those parts of Africa where this began, indeed, it is culturally powerful for men to be promiscuous, but more than that, it is politically powerful for men to use their genitals as a way of expressing their love. Therefore, the disease spread very rapidly. Indeed it is now at such levels in Africa that most of you don't even want to know how bad it is. Certainly those officials don't want to begin to look at the devastating impact of their "sexual prowess."

You need to learn new levels of love, not to give those up. We're not suggesting some sort of celibacy. We're not suggesting some sort of piety where you cannot be sexual. No, please understand: What we're saying is make love something more than just sex, that you don't prove you love someone by the movements of your genitals, that you don't prove your love by activities in bed, sexually, genitally. Rather, you prove your love by that plus additional aspects, additional methods and means of loving.

Open yourself to that particular capacity, to realizing: "Yes, I can express love genitally, but that's not the limit of my love. There are other means. I can express it verbally. I can express it emotionally. I can express it through all levels of actions and all forms of activity." Therefore, learn and begin to stretch into new regions. This is the second meaning of what AIDS is all about.

A Meaning: Learning To Ask for Help

The third: Learn to ask for help. Learn to ask for help — not pity. Learn to ask for help. AIDS is just that. "I need aid." It's a crazy combination of letters that makes one wonder if reality is really real or if it is an illusion. Well, we'll tell you: It's an illusion where such a disease as Acquired Immune Deficiency Syndrome should spell out exactly what it's about, asking for aid! "I need aid. I need help." You need to learn to ask for that help. You see what's happening? Why is it happening in your world now? Why in your world now?

You see, at one time in your world, when information was slower, when the world seemed bigger, when the transportation and communication were limited — and when the amount of destructive ability that you had in your hands was limited — you had time to help yourself, to do for yourself, and you could do it all. A person could learn it all. A person could take care of themselves and never have to rely on, or need, or turn to anyone else.

That situation doesn't exist in your world now. It's too small. Communication is too rapid. Information transfers too quickly, and the dangers of destruction are too imminent for people to be isolated little islands any longer. Chernobyl showed you very clearly that you can clean up all your own nuclear plants if you want. You can carry your placards, and you can close down and change nuclear plants, and do all these sorts of things with safety devices in your own country, but that doesn't protect you from a destructiveness that occurs in another world. In the Soviet Union you can't carry your placards. You can't get them to close down their plants necessarily. Indeed Chernobyl showed you that your world is much smaller than you thought it was.

You need to ask for help. You need to turn to each other. You need to work with each other, not in pity, but in strength and in power, to learn to ask for help. And you need to value yourself, to value yourself enough to realize you are worth it. To ask for help is the third of the messages of AIDS.

A Meaning: Learning To Be Powerful

And the final message is that it is time now in the world for you to learn to be truly powerful. Again, when the world seemed larger and you could create your isolated little pockets, your little villages of existence and belief, your level of power was perhaps not as critical.

But now, as the world is smaller, as your society is more advanced, and as you broach this New Age where each person is going to be more directly and more completely and more consciously responsible for the reality that they create, it is time, people, to truly be powerful, not just to play with the word.

It is time to really begin and to go beyond beginning — to really fulfill and go beyond fulfillment — and really complete being powerful. It is not enough to go to a workshop here and there, to spend a few hours, to spend a few dollars, to learn the techniques, to list the various components of power. It's not enough to read a "how-to" book on intimidation or on manipulation or on some form of domination. It is not enough to develop the art of intimidating and controlling.

It is time to develop the ability to act. It is time to begin to understand and fulfill and complete power, which is the *ability* and the *willingness* to act.

With that, it is time to develop an image of yourself, an image of success. It is time to value yourself, yes, and to image yourself as a successful, powerful being.

These are the messages, messages of defenselessness, of defensiveness, of desperate clinging to the past and desperate desire to know who loves you. These are the meanings: to begin to desire to really know who loves you, to learn new levels and new ways to expand the expression and the experience of — not making love — but expressing love. Learn to ask for help. Value yourself enough to ask not for pity, but for help. Learn now not just to play around with being powerful, but to sincerely learn to be powerful, and develop an image of success.

Belief always precedes reality. Image always precedes reality as well. What you believe and what you image of yourself is what determines the manifestations that you bring forth. These are the meanings. These are the messages.

What do you do about them? The first thing that we can encourage you to do is to take inventory.

An Action: Take Inventory

Take inventory. Where are you on the issues of defenselessness and defensiveness? Are you defenseless, pretending, playing the game, trying to argue and convince yourself and the world that it is so — that it is really true that you are defenseless? Are you totally defensive? Are you shut off? Are you closing yourself off, knowing all the answers, having all the answers, needing nobody, not allowing anybody to help?

Take inventory. Are you desperately, desperately clinging to that past? Are you holding onto angers, blood angers, at your family? Is it worth dying over? Are you so desperately curious to know who loves you that you're willing to give up your life to find out?

Take inventory. End the self-pity that is either your victim or your martyr. End the self-pity. Take personal responsibility for the reality you are creating and for the world reality that is around you. Release your past. Release the anger. Process in whatever way works for you. You can do an express/release meditation. There are various techniques. We've talked of hundreds of them in varieties of ways. Process and let go of that anger. Is it really worth dying over?

An Action: Learn about Love

Learn. Learn as much as you can about love. Learn as much as you can about the giving and the responding and the respecting and the knowing of love. Learn about the humility of intimacy. Learn about the courage of commitment. Learn about the caring. Learn what you can about love, so that you can provide the security, the pleasure, the vulnerability and the trust, so that you can reduce the fear of loss. Feel the caring and the intimacy and the knowing that is love. Learn about it everywhere you can so that you can know how to love, so that you can discern who is loving you, so that you don't have to die for it.

Most of all, people, look at the anger that is saying: "Look what you've done to me." You see, the defenselessness, the defensiveness, the desperateness of the past, and the desperate curiosity to know who loves you all engage and run around an anger that says, "World, you did me wrong. World, look what you did to me!"

Release that anger. Release that rage. Let go of the hurt. We know it is "words to say," but though we don't have time to teach you all of it today, we have talked of these things on numerous occasions. There are methods, there are means, specific ones, to let yourself work with, with which to let yourself grow. Most of you know techniques and methods, or can find them on your own. Let yourself grow. Let yourself learn. Let yourself listen to the messages so that they don't have to continue to be the deadly shouts that they are.

The second thing, beyond taking inventory, is to allow yourself to learn the lessons. Understand the meanings. Bring loving above your Second Chakra. Learn to love from your heart. Learn to love yourself. Learn the varieties and means of loving. You see, sometimes the most difficult loving relationships are those of friendship, because you don't have sex to rely upon. With someone that you can love sexually, often you can show them: "See how much I love you? See how good I was? See how frequently? See how long? See how many orgasms?" Therefore: "How can you question the love?"

But you see, with a friend with whom you are not sexual, you can't fall back upon that sometimes easy, although difficult, method. You rather have to learn other ways of being a friend. Well, similarly it's time not to deny your sexuality, but to expand it. It is time not to deny your loving, but to expand your loving, to find other and alternative means to raise the center of love from the genitals to the heart. That is the lesson. Begin to learn it. Expand the ways you love.

An Action: Learn To Value Yourself

Then begin to value yourself, to value who you are, and realize that you have importance to yourself, and you have importance to other people in your reality. You have importance to other individuals, and you have importance to your world.

You are part of the future that is yet to be born. You are part of a future that is yet to unfold. You play a role, however small, in that future. Start valuing that. You may be but a straw, but you may be a tiny little weight that is going to tip the scales. Do you absolutely know that what you contribute to the world is meaningless? Can you guarantee that you have no value? If you can, all right. But we dare say that you cannot. Let yourself begin to value yourself.

Realize that just maybe, just maybe, an action you take, a book you read, an idea you have, a statement you make may spark, may spur, may begin in someone else's mind solutions to the solutionless problems that so many tell you are around you. Maybe you are the straw that will break the Doom & Gloom's back. Maybe you are the hope. Maybe you are the light. Maybe you are the inspiration. Maybe you are the love that is going to change the course of the future. Don't be so arrogant as to assume that you are not! Be humble enough to allow the possibility that you are, and begin, begin to value yourself.

An Action: Learn What Success Is

Finally, start figuring out what success is for you, and start creating an image of yourself as a successful person. Start seeing yourself in that space. Start letting yourself know and see and live and be success. It doesn't have to mean big cars and fancy clothes. If it does, great, have it. But if it doesn't, let it be what it is.

Let yourself open to an image of what it is for *you* to be successful. As you start working with your success, as you start defining and then developing and expanding and working at what success is, you build an image. Start living that image. Start breathing that image.

Start feeling that image ... but not tangibly! This is where so many go wrong. "Well, my image includes a fancy Mercedes," so they go out and buy it. You can't afford it. No. "My image includes designer clothes, so therefore I have to go get a mortgage." No.

We would suggest if your image includes driving a fancy car, then drive the beat-up Volkswagen that you currently have as though it were a fancy car. Park it sort of cross-angled in the lot (so that no one bumps into it) as though it were a Ferrari. Treat that piece of junk, if you think that's what it is, as though it were an exquisite, valuable foreign automobile.

If indeed your clothes are from J. C. Penney, that modern American designer, let yourself treat them as though they were Givenchy. Let yourself act as though they were Pierre Cardin. Treat them with respect. Don't throw them in the corner as though they're just unworthy! Rather, treat these inexpensive clothes indeed as though they were those expensive designer clothes.

You see, it's not about having the car and having the clothes. It's about the *emotion* that is with it. Create the emotion of success, whether you can actually manifest the trappings yet or not. If you will create the emotion, you will create the trappings. If you will create the emotion, you can create the health to support the trappings, and the success image can be the answer to open you up to your health.

If you have not heard these messages or learned these lessons, does it mean that you absolutely will get AIDS?

No! A thousand times no! A million times! As many times as you need to hear it, no! Absolutely not! But we would suggest that if you have not listened and have not learned, you increase immeasurably your chances of choosing (or letting someone else choose for you) to create this thing called AIDS.

If you clean up your act metaphysically, can you therefore go forth safely knowing you'll never get it? Is it a guarantee? Are we promising you that? No. No. Many thousand times no, absolutely not, no! *Metaphysics does not replace responsibility.* Let us say that again: *Metaphysics does not replace responsibility.* You are responsible. This is not a guarantee that allows you then to carefreely go forth promiscuously. There is no guarantee that you can therefore ignore and, in that sense, almost arrogantly thumb your nose at the messages, at the learnings, at the meanings of this thing. No, metaphysics cannot and does not replace responsibility. You need, and indeed are encouraged, to take the responsibility now.

However, if you will clean up your act physically, and also clean up your act metaphysically, you can create a healthy environment in which you can retard — or if it's too late to stop it, to at least contain — this thing called AIDS, and you can have the potential of knowing that you can create a reality where you have nothing to fear from this particular monster. You can strengthen your physical immune system through various health regimes, particularly if you believe it and know it is true for you.

More importantly, you can strengthen your metaphysical immune system. Then the choices become more conscious. You can decide the future that you desire.

It has been a pleasure talking with you, sharing with you these messages, these meanings. It has been a pleasure touching you, reaching through the words to love you. We do love you.

{At this point on the tape Lazaris provides a beautiful meditation to deal with the messages and meanings of AIDS. Although the meditation is not transcribed here, the tape, with the meditation, is available from the Hay House in Santa Monica, California. Their address is listed in the Acknowledgements section at the front of this book.}

It has been a pleasure working with you, providing for you not a medical device, no, but a metaphysical opportunity. We've enjoyed talking with you, and even more we've enjoyed touching you, reaching you, embracing you, loving you.

We shall close with love, with love, dear one, and peace.

The Hay House, Santa Monica, California

Q: Do you see a medical cure for AIDS coming up anytime soon?

Lazaris: Cure is the wrong word. We would suggest here that there will be a containment. There will be a time when people can contain the spread and the extension of AIDS through medications. Through increased education, understanding, and knowledge this disease can be contained. People will find alternative healing methods that will offer solutions to the destruction.

Will there be a vaccine that will guarantee people that they won't get AIDS? No. Will there be a situation where once someone has contracted it, they can be definitely cured? No. There will be situations where certain health regimens can be instituted whereby the process and progression of AIDS can be reversed, but there will not be a cure or a preventative in the traditional sense.

Beyond the containment, you will adjust and alter your patterns of living and you will create successful, safe environments in which you can go from birth to death without having to be fearing or contracting this kind of devastation.

The search for a remedy will open the door for greater acceptance of alternative healing methods. Those who traditionally ignore the potential of alternative healing will have to pay attention to and consider the real possibilities that alternative approaches to good health may offer.

As researchers frantically seek solutions to AIDS, they will unlock many medical secrets about the immune system and the endocrine system that will lead to breakthroughs in longevity research. Ironically, the disease that threatens and actually does shorten the life of so many will play a significant role in life extension.

No, there will be no cure. You and your researchers make a mistake when you look for the single cure. The consensus reality wants an A + B = C cure that is guaranteed to work. That is the traditional approach to problem solving. Your world will not work with the traditional approaches anymore. This is a New Age. Not only will the solutions be new, but the means of finding those solutions — the approaches — will be new.

There will be no single cure, but there will be many solutions to AIDS. The afflicted will need to search, explore, and experiment to find the solution or solutions that work for them. What works for one may not work for another. Each will have to find their own remedy — their own solution.

There will be many solutions!

Van Ault, **Magical Blend**, *San Francisco*

With love and peace ...

Lazaris

Creating Reality

Q: How
would you
advise us to
manifest our
best reality?

Lazaris: There is a range of best realities. The most difficult choices you have to make are the choices between good things and good things. The choices between good things and bad things are really easy to make. You may offer yourself a range of best choices, say three or four, and that's when it gets tough.

Some say that everything happens for the purposeful good. We suggest in the broadest scope of it, as you back away from it, in the furthest possible way, you can say that, yes, everything happens for the *ultimate* purposeful good. But we dare say that when you're living your life, day in and day out, it's not that way. You create everything that happens, and then you make it good or bad by your choices and your decisions.

How to know what's best for you? There are several qualities that we would encourage you to develop to move toward your best realities. There are seven of them:

First, self-awareness, the realization that you have impact.

Second, self-worth, the understanding that you do *not* have to earn worth, but you have to *uncover* it.

Third, self-esteem, the love that you earn by your honesty, integrity, responsibility, and self-trust.

Fourth, self-love, the love you do not earn. Self-love is given. Establish it by continuously expanding loving yourself. Expand the giving, the caring and the intimacies of love.

Fifth, self-confidence, the ability to cope, the combination of humility and trust, hope and courage to create an energy that is confident — confident that you can deal with your reality.

Sixth, self-respect, which (like self-worth) is not something that you earn, but something that you uncover within yourself. Self-respect is honoring your emotions.

Seventh, self-realization, the realization that you have impact and that you can direct it in the way that you desire. Self-realization is the almost alchemical, synergistic result of developing the other six qualities.

As you develop these seven qualities, you will become the Valuing Self. Self-love is the key, the cornerstone, the most important of them all. As you work with loving yourself, you will instinctively pick those realities that allow you to become more of who you are. As you continuously make growth choices from the foundation of value with the focus of love — which is going to allow you to be the most that you can be — you will direct yourself to the best choices that you can make. You can't go wrong if you continuously use these criteria.

*Alan Vaughan, **Whole Life Monthly**, Santa Monica*

The Paradoxes

Q: Many people, I feel, have difficulty integrating the concept of creating their own reality with the knowledge that there are many people out there, also creating their own realities, and I was wondering, would you shed some light on this paradox?

Lazaris: Certainly so. It is confusing to a lot of people. They say, "Now wait a minute. If I'm creating it and you're creating it, who's really creating it?" There's a sense of male energy competition that gets in there. Whoever's strongest. "If my meditation is stronger than yours, then I get the reality and you don't." No, it doesn't work that way. Reality works in cooperation; it works in harmony. Even the discord in reality works in harmony with other discords of reality to generate a rather strange and, at times, not-at-all-wanted kind of experience.

You as the individual create your whole reality from beginning to end, from morning 'til night, and through the sleep time as well. In your reality everything is an illusion that you are creating, including all the other people with whom you interact. Perhaps a better way to understand it is this: You have written a play — a screenplay, a teleplay, a theatrical play — and not only did you write this play, you also are starring in it, directing it, and producing it. You're going to hire a number of players to act in your particular play. Now they're going to agree to act in your play because it also benefits them, because they also have written a play, you see? In their play, there is a character like you, and in your play there's a character like them.

"I'll play in your play if you'll play in my play." There's an agreement reached.

Here you are, and you've written a play. You create all these other players in your play, some of them major, some of them minor, some of them walk-ons, some of them having lines, and some not having lines.

Some of them play background people in your life — extras, as it were.

There are certain people who are significant, clearly so, people who matter — not more as people, but matter more in terms of the impact that they have on your particular reality.

All right. Those people have all written plays, also. In their plays there's a part for a person just like you, a person that can come in and play that particular role. What we suggest here is that your play and their play mesh. The extent to which they do is the extent to which you are aware of one another.

Let's put it another way: Let's say I'm a person who wants to feel sorry for myself, who wants to go around saying, "The world's against me. No one loves me. No one cares about me. No one treats me good at all." And that's the line I want to say. That's the line I want to say over and over again in my play, and I want to go around trying to convince everybody that it's true.

Well, what kind of players must I have? I can't have players in my play who are exuberant and vibrant, who are giving and loving. I have to surround myself with people who will support my line. Therefore, I will "hire players." I will bring them in and be attracted to those kinds of players who will behave in a way that I can say they are not loving me, not taking care of me, not doing it right for me. Therefore, I get to say my line. I get to feel sorry for myself just like I wanted.

All right, the people that I bring into my play are people who want to feel: "Oh, I'm surrounded by these victims. I'm just surrounded by people who never think I do it good enough. I'm being martyred." And therefore, it meshes. One person feels like a martyr because nobody thinks they do it good enough, and the other person feels like a victim because they're not being treated well enough because nobody ever does it good enough for them. So the two plays mesh.

That's how you create it. In fact, you and others both create it, and it so happens that you both create it such that it meshes together. The victims find the martyrs, and the martyrs find the victims. Those that want to be hurt find those that are willing to be hurtful. Those that want to be loved find those that are willing to be loving. Those that want to laugh find those who are willing to make them laugh.

You may look and say, "Well, now wait a minute, Lazaris. I want to laugh. I want to have fun. I want my life filled with love and joy and happiness. I'm not surrounded by those sorts of people." But if you are not laughing, ask yourself: "Do I really want those things? Do I honestly want to be surrounded by people who are making me laugh, who are making me feel good? Do I honestly want to be surrounded by people who love me?"

Now you see what can happen here: Let's say, "Well, yes, I really want to have people who love me, but I also have an agenda of being a martyr." See, those are contradictions. You may want to be surrounded by laughter and love, but if you want to be a martyr more, which reality do you suppose you will create?

So if you find yourself in a position where you want love in your life, but you don't have it, you first need to look, using meditation, to find out: "Do I really want love in my life?" Then find out: "Are there some contradictory wants and desires that I have? Are there inconsistent wants and desires that I have?" If so, then you need to eliminate them. If not, then you need to reinforce the fact that you really do want love in your life. The bottom line is you don't always create what you *ask* for, but you always create what, at some level, you *want*.

Now comes in the question: What about starving children? Are you telling me that they want to starve?

No. No. No. No. No, we're not suggesting that at all. We're not suggesting that people who are in desperate states in this world, starving in Ethiopia, or in any part of the world, are wanting it in that conscious way.

We're not suggesting that those Black people in South Africa want to get killed, want to have their families destroyed. But what we will suggest is this: On a certain level they are creating it. They may not be verbally conscious of that creation yet. They may not have the intellectual awareness, the knowledge, of how they are creating it yet, but they are creating it on a level for some reason. Whether they want it or not, they don't think they *deserve* any better. They don't think they're entitled to any better.

*"That other parts of the world are not ready to work with self-created reality doesn't mean it's **not** self-created."*

Additionally, they might think that such tragedy, such misery, might be a way for them to give, might be a way for them to perhaps inspire those more fortunate to take more responsibility for those less fortunate. Because you are aware of their plight, they might be choosing their pain to inspire you to reach out to them and to help them — to teach them how to end pain — to end their pain, perhaps to end all pain. They may have their own agenda that we would not presume that you should understand.

They indeed are creating it by *allowing* that reality to occur. Now perhaps with education, perhaps with understanding, perhaps with lots of love and lots of support, and indeed in many cases with lots of food, they could then take the time to figure out why they thought they deserved that reality, why they thought they didn't deserve any better.

Maybe they can be shown that they could create a more beneficial reality for themselves. We aren't suggesting to teach them how to meditate right off. We're suggesting feed them, take care of them, give them a sense of stability, meet some of their basic needs. Once those needs are met, then let's sit down and learn about meditation. Then let's sit down and learn about metaphysics. Then let's combine the metaphysics and the meditation to create a better reality for everyone.

But let's not start there. First let's feed them. Let's take care of them. Let's get rid of their illness. Let's give them the resources that they need, the help that they need, and the support that they need to get their lives working. Then, once the needs are met, we can start looking for the esoterics.

You see, in your world, most of your needs are met. As a society, you can afford to work with the esoterics. Those esoterics say: Each person creates their own reality. That others in the world are not yet able to work with the esoterics doesn't mean that they're not true. That other parts of the world are not ready to work with self-created reality doesn't mean that it's *not* self-created.

Lee Perry, Van Nuys, California

Lazaris: First of all, there's nothing over which you have no control. "Oh, yes, there is! Yes, there is!" Well, if you can convince yourself of it, you have that option. But we suggest here that there is nothing over which you have no control. You do create it all. No asterisks, no fine print, no hidden meanings. You do create it all. You create it two ways: Either you cause things to occur, by your choice, by your decision, by the feelings that you have, by the thoughts that you hold, by your attitudes and by your beliefs — you cause things to occur — or else you allow them.

Q: You said a person is responsible for everything that happens to him. How can a person be responsible for things over which he has no control?

Now, we would agree: You did not cause the airplane crash that ... You did not cause that. You weren't the one who jimmied with the flaps over Detroit and made that plane crash, clearly not. You didn't program it. You weren't sitting there thinking, "I hope a plane crashes. I hope a plane crashes." No, you didn't cause it. You are not aware of any particular choices or any particular decisions you made vis-à-vis that airplane crash — nor did you have any thoughts or any feelings about that particular plane, nor did you have any particular attitudes or beliefs about that plane.

But you did allow that reality to occur. We would encourage you to look at why. "Why did I allow it?" Was it to support a belief that it's getting more dangerous to fly every day? Was it to support a belief of "what's this world coming to?" Was it to support a belief in tragedy and that things have to go that way? Was it to scare yourself about your next air flight?

What impact did that crash have upon you? For some of you it had no impact whatsoever. "Oh, another plane went down. What airline was it? What airline was it?" For some of you it touched you very deeply. The sadness of it, and the fact that it was such human error as not adjusting the flaps properly, had true impact upon you.

Therefore, we suggest, you allowed it for varying reasons — your reasons. How can you create your reality when there are things that happen "beyond your control?" By allowing them to occur. By allowing them to occur in your reality.

You didn't cause those people to be kidnapped in the Middle East. You didn't cause those acts of terrorism directly. But you allowed them into your reality, and you allowed them in because you wanted to learn something or show yourself something about yourself. You wanted to show yourself something or learn something about yourself. Maybe it was your reaction to those who don't follow the rules. (Third World nations never seem to follow the rules of war and peace.) Maybe it was to create tension in your life. Maybe it was to feel sadness. Maybe that's why you created it, because you wanted to feel that sadness. Now admittedly the people who were kidnapped had a much more active part in the creation, but you allowed it.

Example: There was the circumstance of a couple who had been waiting numbers of years to have their baby. She was a special education teacher and dealt with those special children who have learning disabilities. He worked with handicapped children. Both of them were educators, very highly regarded. They had their child. The child was born with mental retardation. They were devastated.

The reason that that reality was created, in that way, which they came to realize and understand, was that they were insecure about their ability to love. They knew they could love handicapped children, but they didn't know if they could love a child without handicaps.

The infant in this case had her particular reasons for being so handicapped and agreed: "OK, you want to give birth to a child. Because of the fear, you have a belief or a creation here of bringing in a handicapped child. I want to be handicapped for various reasons, so therefore your creation and my creation fit together, and therefore they overlap, and thus we join together." Now their reasons may be miles and miles and miles apart, but for a number of reasons they overlapped, so the child was born handicapped. It was the child's choice and the parents' choice, for quite different reasons. In that regard the energies can fit together.

When, indeed, you involve yourself with a person, and that's their reality, that's what they're creating, it is in your reality because for some reason it overlaps. For some reason it overlaps. When you can consciously create your reality fully and completely, then there will be minimal surprises as to who and what you create in your reality. You do create it all. The people you attract to you are the people that you choose to attract to you.

We use another analogy: Let us say there are two of you who are going to swim a race, and there's a third person, a third one of you who is going to watch. On your mark ... get set ... bang! Go! Who wins? Whoever decides to win — not the stronger, not the better, not the more powerful programmer. Each person creates their own reality.

"Well, does it mean that if two of us want the same job we both get it? Yes ..."

Person A decides, "I'm going to win." And if they really do make that decision, they will win, and in their reality Person B loses, and the person in the stands has the same thought.

"Who won?"

"You did! What are you asking such a silly question for?"

Person B, however, may have other ideas in their personal reality, and they're saying, "I'm going to win." And if they really believe that and really know that, then they win and Person A loses, and the person in the stands ...

"Who won?"

"Well, you did, of course. What a silly question you ask!"

And indeed we would even go further to suggest that the person in the stands, who is also a participant, not really an observer, has their own honest expectation of who is going to win. In their reality the winner is the one that they choose, decide upon, feel, think, and have attitudes and beliefs about. Therefore, some think there are potentially only two winners, because there are only two swimmers, but we suggest that there are three realities that fit together.

Now sometimes what happens is Person A expects to win, and they really do expect to win, whereas Person B expects to win but has a hidden agenda of "losing once again." And Person C has an agenda of saying that "A is the better swimmer, so they'll probably win!" It may well work that in all three people's realities Person A wins. We would suggest here that in that sense all three realities may congeal. All three realities may pinpoint on the singular incident. Did A win or not? And all three may agree: "Yes, A won," one says happily, one says sadly, one says confidently.

But if they don't all agree, then the realities don't converge. There are many converging and many non-converging realities in the whole of it all.

Well, does that mean if two of us are wanting the same job we could both get it? Yes, it does mean that. But, you see, in your set you will be the one who gets it or does not get it, and everybody else will agree with you, because everybody else in your set will see it your way. Everyone else in your set is in your set!

There are different sets. You cannot be aware of *that* set because you're in *this* set, and that's the way you create your reality. It's all your creation, and there is a multiplicity of universes, a multiplicity of realities, all existing from one moment to the next. You pull them together, you edit the film of your realities, and you call *this* one real. That's how it fits together.

Anonymous Question, Seattle Evening with Lazaris, 1987

Lazaris: Well, that is a dilemma. Indeed, you create your whole reality. Part of the solution to that dilemma is the fact that you create two ways. One is by causing things. You cause things to happen. Indeed, you create them actively. And the other way is by allowing. You allow things to happen in your reality. So indeed to say, "Hey, look, there are starving people in Africa!" And you know what? There are starving people right here in Los Angeles, too. You say there are starving people out there. You created that. Did you cause it? No, but you are allowing it. You are allowing it.

The question for you to look at is why. "Why am I allowing this reality of starvation? Why am I allowing the reality of hearing of plane crashes, or hearing of people dying of various diseases? Why am I hearing of these human disasters or individual disasters? They are not happening to me, but why am I hearing of them?"

As you will look at why — why you are allowing, why you are bringing it into your reality — you can learn from that and experience it for yourself.

Q: I'm having a little bit of confusion about people suffering and starving. On one hand I'm creating my own reality, and I've come here to learn certain lessons. Others have come here to learn their lessons. At what point is it infringing on their reality, and the lessons they come into this incarnation to learn, when I go and help them?

"Now the reason for starvation is ..." There is no "reason" for starvation! There is one person's reason, and there is another's reason, and there is your personal reason. So many in metaphysics want to generalize: "All starvation means ..." No. Starvation is not a generic symbol. Starvation is personal, and it hurts. Some of you are creating it because you want to help, because you want to go there, because you want to reach out and touch people, because you want to help in that way. And therefore, you are allowing it. You are not causing it. You are allowing it. You need permission and a concrete reason to love and care.

"If you've got a chance to help, do it. If you've got a chance to reach out, do it. If you've got a chance to love, never pass up the opportunity."

Others, in that sense, are allowing it because you want to help in a more distant way. Some of you are allowing it because you are still dealing with a reality of scarcity. You still believe that there is a limited amount of food, a limited amount of resource, a limited amount of love. And we suggest that as you can really learn, not all of you, but as you can realize that there's enough love to go around, there's more than enough love to go around, then you will start healing that energy that in your reality is called starvation or scarcity.

We have related this before, but it's an important point. There was a drought in the Southeast, and a lot of the Doom and Gloom people, a lot of the erudite, very sophisticated, metaphysical West Coast people, said, "Aha! Look! It starting! See? I told you! The end is coming. The end's coming. The end's going to happen! See, look at that drought. See, just like they said: drought. See, they're starving to death. They're starving. Their animals are dying. Look at that starvation. Look at that. This is going to be the worst ever. Oh, it's the beginning of the end. It's the beginning of the end!"

Some farmer (yes, some farmer) was watching his television and said, "No, I can't stand seeing those people go through that. I wonder what I can do to help."

And he sent hay, bales of hay. And other farmers, not the Farm Bureau, not the Government on Health, Education and Welfare, no, not the bureaucracy, but individual men and women who do not know metaphysics from anything, but know love, reached out.

They gathered together their hay, and they sent it to that area of the world. While many of the oh-know-it-so-well metaphysicians were *pointing* fingers in blame, those not-so-knowing metaphysicians were *lifting* fingers in love.

If you've got a chance to help, do it. If you've got a chance to reach out, do it. If you've got a chance to love, never pass up the opportunity. Always reach out, because that may be why you are creating it. You can't figure it out, and sometimes it's not your place even to begin to try to figure out why they might be creating a tragic reality, but you reach, you love, you care, and there's never a point where you stop. There is never a point where you stop.

Always reach, always love. If there comes a point where it becomes apparent that no, they want to die, or they want to continue the starvation, they will manage to work around your love.

Don't stop sending love. Don't stop giving love. Don't stop! Never!

Anonymous Question, Whole Life Expo, Los Angeles, 1987

Generating Success

Q: I'm a successful businessman. Why am I not as successful as Ted Turner and Donald Trump? ... {laughter} ... If I program and they don't, did they choose their life before birth?

Lazaris: You are successful, and why aren't you as successful as they are when you program and they don't? Who said they don't? Who said they don't program?

Maybe they don't program in the same way you do, but we can tell you Ted Turner programs — not in the way he would call metaphysical, but you can be sure he has Dreams. He has desires, and he has expectations, and he has an imagination that would startle many of you. He knows he makes his own choices, and, you know, for sure he's aware that he makes decisions, and that it's his feelings and his thoughts and his beliefs that are in the way. You know that when he fails he's not blaming other people. He is taking the responsibility himself. Oh, yes, publicly he may point many a finger, but he's taking the responsibility himself privately. The man goes to sleep at night dreaming about the reality he wants to create. He's programming, probably more hours a day than you would be willing to.

And Donald Trump? His whole thing, Trump Tower. Do you have any idea how many years he could *taste* that project, how many years he dreamt of it, how many years he "lived" this burning desire to have that whole block, to buy up all that property and piece by piece by piece to put it together? What patience! Sure, he had money and all that, but beyond that, the Dream was there. You'd better believe he programs.

The super successful — not people who just inherited a great deal of wealth, but people who made a great deal of wealth — they're Dreamers, every last one of them. They're Dreamers, and they're programmers. Oooh, they program. They don't necessarily sit down and close their eyes and go into meditation. They program with their eyes open walking down the hall, driving the car, reading the newspaper, at dinner, at dinner parties, etc. They program every day, all day long. With some, it's called "driven." With some it is driven, and that can be unfortunate. But they do program.

First of all, you are a successful businessman. Yes, you are. And the reason you're not as successful as they are is that you haven't dreamed big enough. You haven't dreamed big enough.

Now, should you? No, not necessarily. Not necessarily. Not everybody is going to become a Donald Trump. If you all owned a whole block of New York City, it would be rather a strange and boring city, wouldn't it? ... {laughter} ... You see, for Donald Trump, that's what was important to him. To you, your level of success may be just great. "Hey, I'm happy with it. I'm not looking to be the richest man in the world. I'm not looking to own half of New York City. I'm not looking for that level of visibility. I want enough success that I can be happy."

You see, Donald Trump isn't doing the other things that maybe you are. Ted Turner isn't doing, we know, some of the other things you are doing. It's a matter of allocation. To be totally successful does not mean being another Ted Turner. No. You have other priorities that fit in there. You have other priorities.

You're not dreaming that big, with your desire, expectation and imagination, and maybe that's best. Maybe there are other areas that you have Donald Trump and Ted Turner beat seven ways to Sunday. You've got something in your life, such as a spirituality, that they don't have, that they don't have. And we know it's true, as well.

You see, you can be metaphysical without being spiritual. It's hard to be spiritual without being metaphysical, but we suggest that you can be metaphysical without being spiritual.

There are people out there, for example, who are creating all kinds of success. We talk about consciously creating success, right? There are people out there who are very, very successful, and they don't know how they got there. "That's unfair, Lazaris! Why do I have to know, and they don't!" You don't have to, but, you see, the choice comes: "Is this going to be a spiritual lifetime for you or not?" Some people are creating tremendous amounts of success and haven't the foggiest idea how. That's fine. This may be an R & R lifetime for them. They don't have to have fun. They don't have to consciously create their success.

But if you want to be spiritual, if you want to accomplish your goal, if you want to fulfill your focuses, your purposes, your mission, your task, whatever you call it, then it is important that you do those things. And therefore maybe someone will have even more consensus reality success than you. But you will be more successful, because you're consciously doing it, and you're having fun.

Is Donald Trump having fun? Yeah, he's having fun. ... {laughter} ... And he's pretty conscious of why he's creating his reality. Ted Turner's having fun most of the time. A lot of people who are successful are having fun. A lot of them don't know how they did it, though. They don't know how they did it. But don't assume that just because they don't use the same vernacular as you that they're not metaphysical or spiritual or programming.

Look at yourself: Do you really want to be them? If you do, why? Why is it important? Why do you want that level?

You find your level, what works for you, and that's what you aspire to. That's your success. Well, bravo! Do you really want to be Ted Turner? No, you don't. Do you know why? Because you're not him. ... {laughter} ... If you wanted to be Ted Turner, you could have been Ted Turner. If you wanted to be Donald Trump, you could have been Donald Trump.

People say, "Oh, look at that! Look at So-and-So. Oh, I wish I had money. I wish I were born rich!" No, you don't. You could have been. There are a lot of very rich people who are barren, who would have loved to have kids. You could have been born to a Rockefeller. There's enough of 'em! ... {laughter} ... They have kids. Somebody's born into that money. You didn't want to be. Why? That's for you to figure out, perhaps, but if you really wanted to be Ted Turner you would have been.

You wanted to be you. Don't aspire to ever be anybody else but you. So don't try to be Ted Turner or Donald Trump. Be you. Find the level of success where you can have the balance, and reach that. Therefore, dream a little bigger than you're dreaming, but not as big as that, because you have other dreams to dream. And we know your energy: You have other dreams to dream that those men aren't dreaming. Dream *your* dreams.

Anonymous Question, Atlanta Evening with Lazaris, 1987

Q: You often said that if one doesn't get what one programs for, one doesn't really want it, or has a hidden agenda for not allowing oneself what one wants.

Others in the metaphysical community have said that if your programming isn't working, it's because God has something else in mind for you. Is this a copout answer only, or is it ever appropriate?

Lazaris: It's mostly a copout answer, but can be appropriate from time to time. We suggest you get what you want. This is an illusion. This is an illusion. You can have as much Silly Putty as you want. ... {laughter} ... Absolutely. It is all an illusion. It's your game.

"God, can I have a car?"

"Yes."

"Can I have a fancy car?"

"Yes."

It's just Silly Putty. It's Silly Putty. What would be the best possible reality? What could be better than getting what you honestly want? God doesn't necessarily have anything better in store for you than what you want. Your reality is an illusion. You get what you want, but not always what you ask for. When you program and it doesn't work, it can mean a number of things. It means that you do have hidden agendas. You're taking payoffs, or you have other agendas. Also, it could mean you're not clear in your programming — you're not clear on definition of terms or the semantics of what you and your subconscious interpret (you're not on the same wavelength). Further, there are faulty programmings.

Even if you're using our techniques, which work rather incredibly well, you can do them improperly. If you do a 33-second technique for 35 seconds, for example, it's going to change the energy — not bring failure necessarily, it's not black and white — but it's not going to be the same as if you do it for 33 seconds. If you're not feeling a full sense of bliss, if you're just going ho-hum, ho-hum, ho-hum for 33 seconds, then it's certainly not going to create the same reality.

It could mean that you're not using your tools, you're not using the resources, and it could mean that indeed other things of that sort are going on — that you don't really want what you ask for, or you don't have the beliefs and the attitudes to allow it.

Upon occasion your Higher Self will intercede. Your Higher Self will know, for example, that "if they get that, it's going to set them back in their growth." At times God, through your Higher Self, will intercede, but it's not as though God says you can't have something. You can have it all. Your Higher Self and God, through your Higher Self, may be acting for your benefit — on your behalf — and intercede.

For example: "I want to program a lot of money so I can quit work." Your Higher Self knows that will kill you, and therefore, in your interest, may well, for that very reason, interfere with your programming. If your motivations aren't clear and aren't harmonious and aren't productive, then SOMETIMES — SOMETIMES — SOMETIMES your Higher Self will step in. NOT VERY OFTEN.

A lot of people say: "Oh, it's God's will, the purposeful good." They are discounting the whole possibility of a negative ego.

Anonymous Question, Seattle Evening with Lazaris, 1987

Q: Your manifesting techniques are pretty popular these days with the metaphysical movement. How are your techniques of manifesting and programming different than what a lot of other people are teaching, and what kinds of results are people getting from them?

Lazaris: Well, it's difficult to answer in terms of how they are different from others because many others aren't offering any technique at all, and therefore we would suggest perhaps the first difference is that with us techniques exist as opposed to with others they do not.

So often in this field one is told, "You need to love yourself more, you need to be more self-confident. You need more of this. You need more of that." But you're never told how to do it. You're told, "Just do it. Just sit down and meditate on it. Just let it happen." That is often unfulfilling, for indeed you go to a workshop, you go seeking advice, because you already know you don't love yourself enough.

Just being told isn't necessarily going to help you. You need to know specific techniques of how to do that. Also, you are told you create your own reality, but very few tell you exactly how to go about doing it. What are the steps? What are the procedures? And even fewer would tell you why the procedures work. The first major difference of our techniques is the very fact that they exist as opposed to that they don't exist.

Beyond that, there are programming techniques, and there are "how-to" books. There are books on all kinds of self-help topics. The difference between our techniques and those is the workability. The techniques we recommend do work. Part of the reason they work is because the techniques we offer give power back to you. They do not take power from you.

We do not talk about techniques in mystical terms of "just do it because we said so." We explain how and why and where to use them, what the configurations are, and what the factors are so as to produce the results that are important to you. Therefore, you aren't just doing a technique as some sort of ritual. You're doing a technique with a presence of understanding, and with the presence of power.

The difference also between our techniques and those of others is that our techniques incorporate responsibility, wherein it's not just "do this and you'll get what you want" without any sense of ownership, without any sense of impact, without any sense of responsibility. Very clearly you are responsible for what you're creating, for your success or your failure, with the various techniques.

Those are some of the differences.

In terms of what the impact has been, we would suggest here that is difficult to say other than to suggest that Concept: Synergy, the organization through which we operate, has received thousands of letters from people amazed that the techniques work. They've read books. They've tried this. They've tried that. They've done various techniques before, and almost given up on the possibility that the techniques would have any kind of impact. Then they try one more time, and to their amazement, to their joy, to their celebration, they find that indeed it works.

"Some people erroneously think the technique is what produces the results. In fact, they produce the results using the technique as a way of amplifying their own intention..."

There is no particular category of techniques that works better than any other. There have been incredible successes, from people who have allowed themselves grand healings of terminal blood diseases, of tumors that were recorded by doctors and were to be operated upon within days that suddenly have disappeared, of back problems, of nerve distresses, of broken bones, of crushed vertebrae, and various other things that have all been healed. This is not true with absolutely every person, but people have allowed the techniques to work in the areas of healing.

Indeed with monies, jobs and contractual things, tangible things of this sort, miracles have been allowed to occur. Negotiations of contracts and things of this sort have been beautifully impacted and augmented by various techniques.

Some people erroneously think the technique is what produces the results. In fact, *they* produce the results using the technique as a way of focusing, using the technique as a way of amplifying their own intention, their own desire, their own imagination and their own expectation.

The techniques have thus allowed them to generate the reality that they wanted. How many people are there? Thousands. Tens of thousands. The numbers are perhaps not as important as the fact that indeed people are allowing themselves to realize that creating your own reality is not just a theory, that creating your own reality is not just something you talk about but don't know how to do. It is specific. It is very powerful. It is very actual.

Creating your own reality doesn't mean that you only create your responses to what happens to you in the world. It means that you create what actually happens to you in the world quite personally and quite directly. The impact of realizing this truth — the result of practicing techniques and using manifesting techniques literally to manifest realities — is that people say, "It couldn't have happened any other way — the techniques worked. I worked!" It has brought them face to face with encountering or confronting the energy of realizing, "I guess I do really, literally create my own reality. There are no asterisks. There is no fine print. I do it myself."

*Van Ault, **Magical Blend**, San Francisco*

The Magic of Processing

Lazaris: Start right away, as soon as you process. Look at it, and as soon as you feel you're getting there, go ahead and use the techniques. They're not going to hurt you. If you haven't done enough processing, the feedback will come in the fact that you won't create the reality. How much processing is enough processing? As long as it's solid processing, continue. As soon as it dwindles, as soon as it diminishes, as soon as you can't go any further, then start using your techniques, start working with them.

Q: How do I know when I've done enough processing before I start using the techniques for creating abundance?

If you know, for example, that you have a major problem with self-pity, work it through. Do the techniques. Do the releasing. Handle it. Therefore, "There, I've done it. Now, let me do the techniques." You do the techniques. They work a little bit, and then they don't work. What do you feel? "Well, I'm feeling just really sorry for myself!" ... {laughter} ... "Maybe I'm not done with self-pity yet, eh?" ... {laughter} ... Right.

So you go back to the drawing board, and you work some more and see what's going on, what's the hold up, what's the hang-on, and what's the blockage. And there! "I think I've got it. I think I've got it."

So you go back and you start using the techniques, or you use them all along while you're processing — don't ever stop. You start creating some successes. It just gets going well, and you're starting to count on it, and it flattens out again. "Oh, I just don't know what's wrong with me. Could it be I'm in self-pity?" Yeah. Back to the drawing board.

"Self-love isn't something that shows up on your 'to do' list."

You process until you are done, but we encourage you to use the techniques in the meantime. Yes, do a legitimate job with the processing, but then start applying the techniques. Start working with them. If the abundance is coming, keep checking, keep working with it. It's a process/grow, process/grow situation.

When does it ever end? When you're done. When you're done. Well, when's that? When *you* decide.

You can process through this lifetime and through any number of lifetimes, hundreds of lifetimes in a row. Nobody up there is going to say, "Hey, Bunkie, you're done." … {laughter} … You say, "I'm done. I'm walking away from my self-pity. I'm letting go of the past. I'm going to stop avoiding the responsibility and the joy of success. I'm going to give up blaming. I'm going to give up my righteousness. I'm going to create my own reality now." When *you* decide.

When we talk of empowerment, one of the secrets of empowerment is that change only occurs now. You don't change in the past. You don't change in the future. *You change now.*

And we'll tell you something your egos aren't going to like to hear: Any process that you do with legitimacy can be well underway within 20 minutes. Then you can begin programming, and creating your reality the next moment, or the next ten thousand moments, whenever you choose. Your reality is *your* creation.

If you loved yourself enough, you wouldn't have to do any techniques. If you loved yourself totally, you wouldn't even have to go to school, because any information you needed would be available to you. Your subconscious knows what 2 x 2 and 10 x 10 is. Your subconscious knows that George Washington was the first President. For crying out loud, you may have been alive during that time!

Your unconscious mind has a raft of information about all your previous and future lifetimes, and your Higher Consciousness knows everything. If you truly loved yourself enough, you wouldn't even have to learn how to write or read books, because whatever information you needed could just be pulled in. You wouldn't need to process. You wouldn't need to program. You wouldn't need the 33-second technique or candle technique or color technique. You wouldn't need any of that — not even the Causal Plane — none of it. You would just say, "I want this. I'm choosing this. I believe this and am making these choices." Bing! Bing! Bing! It's there.

However, the fact of the matter is, you don't love yourself enough yet. Thus, rather than sit around twidling your thumbs waiting for that love to somehow happen, process, program and work on continuously improving your level of self-love. Someday you will love yourself enough, and then you can stop processing and programming.

Until that day, don't sit on the sidelines. "Well, I'm waiting to love myself enough," because, you see, the steps of getting there are the qualities of being there, and the qualities of being there are the steps to get there. Therefore, if you sit on the sidelines, you will never love yourself enough. In the meantime, in the in-between time, program, process, work, grow, stretch, but never forget to love yourself, and never forget to add to that self-love always....

Self-love isn't something that shows up on your "to do" list. "Oh, I did self-love a year ago." ... {laughter} ... Self-love is something you do every single day of your life. Each day love yourself a little more if you can, and if you can't today, tomorrow love yourself a little more and a little more and a little more.

Will you ever reach the point in this lifetime where you love yourself enough? You will get to the point in this lifetime — not all of you, we hasten to say, unfortunately — but many of you will get to the point where you love yourself enough that you can start using more and more the "techniqueless" technique.

More and more we're teaching "techniqueless" techniques where you demand, where you give permission, where you allow miracles — miracles being those successful realities that are much more than you expect them to be. More and more of you who have been working with your growth with a sincerity are getting beautifully close to really developing techniqueless techniques of reality creation. You are getting beautifully close to loving yourself more than "good enough."

Now even when you're done with this lifetime, you won't stop then. You are perpetually working on loving yourself. We are continuously working on loving ourselves. We are continuously growing. We wouldn't stop for a moment. It's just too much fun. Now admittedly, we don't process out our mother and our father, because we don't have a mother and father. And we don't process out our anger and our fear and our doubt, because we don't have anger, fear, or doubt. We don't process. We create. We don't program, but in the workshops and seminars, we program *with* you. In our reality, we are continuously growing, always becoming more of who we are, always discovering more of the pieces of God that we are, just as you are. But you have the particular encumbrance and the particular beauty of a body and a physical illusion. We don't.

" ... miracles being those successful realities that are much more than you expect them to be."

Anonymous Question, Seattle Evening with Lazaris, 1987

Lazaris: At a certain point you aren't able to consciously know or consciously take responsibility for the reality you create. Please understand, a child does create their own reality, absolutely so. But, you see, they aren't in a position to be able to be fully responsible for that. Suppose you have an infant, for example. You put their clothes on, and you dress them, and you put their little socks on, and you put on their little shoes, and you tie those little shoes and this sort of thing.

Q: How would you suggest we deal with children in helping them understand that they create their own reality?

Then they get a little older and you put on a little bigger clothes and a little bigger shoes, and at a certain point they tell you, "No! No! I want to do it! I want to do it!" They begin, in that particular sense, wanting to dress themselves. Don't they do a terrible job of it, too! ... {laughter} ... But they want to do it themselves, and they may spend 20 minutes, 30 minutes tying a shoe that would take you only moments to do.

"Come on, we're running late."

"I want to tie my own shoe!"

What they're basically saying is: "I want to start taking some of that responsibility," and therefore you say, "OK, dress yourself." You explain to them why the buttons need to line up and show them a way to do that. You explain why you need to put the left shoe on this foot, you see, and the right shoe on this foot, because it's more comfortable that way, and you don't look so weird ... {laughter} ... and why it is important to tie your shoe like this so that it stays tied. You teach them and you teach them, and pretty soon they're able to do it just fine. By the time they get to be 20 or so, why they can dress themselves ... {laughter} ... usually fairly accurately.

When do you have them take responsibility? Admittedly, at age two if they fall down and get hurt, you don't say, "Well, why did you do this? Why have you created this reality?" Clearly not. You pick them up, you kiss them, you hug them, and you make it better, absolutely so.

But by the time children are age seven, they're able to start taking some of that responsibility. Then if they fall down and scrape their knee, you pick them up, you hug them, you make it better, and then you start talking about, "I wonder why you did that? I wonder why you thought you needed to fall down? I wonder what you were trying to create there?" You don't demand or insist, as you might with an adult, but as they grow older and you talk of responsibility, you give them that option, that choice of seeing it. That way, they will learn. There are certain mothers that we've worked with over a number of years who are raising their children very much in this way, starting at about age seven.

There is a particular woman who has a daughter whom she's been raising with the concept of taking responsibility. The daughter, now age 13, has the maturity of an 18-year-old. She rather looks at her reality as "why did I create this? Oh, look, I'm being a victim here. Look at the self-pity. Can you believe that? I see why I didn't do well on that. I was angry at you, and I was punishing you for this and that and the other." She is talking in those terms, not just as rhetoric, but really meaning and understanding what she says.

Now that doesn't mean she's perfect. She can be absolutely obnoxious, as any teenager can be, but when she's in the mood, she's able to take that responsibility and actively see herself creating her reality. Hopefully, when she gets a little older and moves through her adolescence and into adulthood, she will still maintain her zeal for that responsibility.

Some people wonder if we mean it when we say that an infant creates their own reality. "Are you telling me an infant child is responsible for their illnesses!?" Yes. We suggest they are, but not as the infant child.

When an infant is born, there is a very mature soul inside of that little, tiny body. That's why birth is such a trauma, because prior to birth you, as a consciousness, were a free spirit able to do and be anything. Then suddenly you found yourself contained in this funny little body. That's a trauma, absolutely. That's why, in the first several months, you just go to sleep, and you sleep most of the time. "Ooh! I can't deal with this!" ... {laughter} ... "Did I do this?"

Sometimes children decide, "Yeah, and I made a mistake," and they die early. Crib deaths are seldom due to mother's negligence or anything of that sort, clearly not. You can't blame everything on mom. Sometimes the consciousness realizes, "I made a mistake." Sometimes that mistake was just the realization that "I was born too soon or too late." Sometimes the realization is "these parents aren't going to give me the amount of trauma that I want in my life."

You know, some of you decided that you wanted to grow up and really experience guilt. So you picked those parents because they make you feel guilty! Would they heap it on! Did they do a job! But, you see, you might have been born and realized, "These parents aren't going to make me feel guilty enough. They're going to be too loving, too understanding. I made a mistake. I had better back out. So therefore, how can I do that?"

They create illnesses. Therefore, at that level, it is not so much that the *infant* is responsible, but that the *consciousness* is. Therefore, you don't hold them accountable, but indeed you understand the reality that is being manifested. Those things always mesh together as well.

Sometimes an infant decides, a soul decides, a consciousness decides, "Oops, I goofed. I made a mistake. This isn't the right lifetime. You're not the right people." They choose to back out through illness or some sort of tragic death.

The parents, on some level, have agreed to allow that to occur. As the mother or father of such a child, there is a level of agreement. We're not saying that they necessarily fully consciously decided, "OK, you should die now." But we do suggest that on some level they made that decision that they would allow that infant the opportunity to leave again. The parents would not demand, "You're here. You stay." They love enough to let go. Does that make sense? All right, fine.

Anonymous Question, Seattle Evening with Lazaris, 1988

The Role of Destiny

Q: If you have a destiny, where does reality creation fit in? To what extent does destiny predetermine your reality?

Lazaris: You do have a destiny, if you so choose. This is how it fits together: There is no sense of predetermination in the fullest extent of that word. Your life is not really mapped out for you. It's not laid out so neatly. What is true is that between lifetimes you, as a consciousness, go through a whole lot of growth. You experience the death process, being dead, going to heaven and those sorts of things.

Then you get tired of it and realize, "Is this all there is?" Then all the backdrops fall away, and you get to work. You start reviewing the lifetime that you finished. You review it in retrospect and in relationship to the other lifetimes that are all concurrent. Then you decide whether you want to move through your growth without returning to physical form or if you want to pick another lifetime to experience.

In that process of picking another lifetime, what happens is that you create broad strokes. You decide you want to learn about this, and this, and this, and you want to experience that. You create what we call the broad strokes of your life, the broad, sweeping gestures in your energy. Then you enter into this life. Your consciousness, your massive consciousness, all of a sudden confines itself in this infant body, and you then forget all of what went before. You don't remember. Well, some children do remember for awhile, but they soon forget. The amnesia sets in, and they forget.

You have these broad strokes in your life. You decide, for example, "I'm going to come from a broken home. I'm going to have a broad, sweeping illness here." Or, "I'm going to grow up and deal with love in such a way as to have several very hurtful relationships." You decide on these broad strokes. You also have things you want to accomplish in the lifetime. "I want to learn this and accomplish that, and I want to be of service in this way or that way, or whatever." But every moment you can change it.

For example, maybe you put a broad, sweeping stroke in your life that you were going to have a tragic accident and be crippled. As you approach that time, you change your mind. "I don't want to do 'tragic accident.' I'm going to change it." You don't have the tragic accident, and then your whole lifetime changes, absolutely it does.

You have the free will, at any moment, either to accept the predecided, sweeping generalities in your life, or to change them. If you accept the broad, sweeping generalities, you still have to fill in the day-in and day-

"You have free will, at any moment, either to accept the predecided, sweeping generalities in your life, or to change them."

out existence where indeed you exert your free will, where you create the reality.

You see, you are the one who is creating the broad strokes, and therefore you can change them. When we talk with many of you, as well you know, we psychically tell you what's going to be happening, what you're creating, what you're generating. Basically what we're telling you is the blueprint that you've laid out for yourself. You have decided what you are going to create, and therefore you've laid out a blueprint, like an architect.

We look at your blueprint, and we tell you: "Now you've done this, and it looks like that, and this is what's going to happen next June and in two years from now. That's when this energy is going to shift, and then you're going to open up to that in five years." You can either say, "I like that" and go ahead with your blueprint, or you can say, "Yuck! I don't want that," and then change your blueprint. You can say, "I like it, but I want it to come sooner," or "I want it to come later" and thus adjust the blueprint.

Therein lies the value of seeing your future, of understanding what you've got laid out for yourself, because sometimes you're so close to your blueprint that you can't always see for yourself what's going on. You could if you really wanted to look, if you wanted to develop that expertise to see, you could, but often you don't.

As we lay out a future for people, it is not absolute — it is only probable. You are the decision maker. Just as you may have chosen this or that or the other, you can change it.

That's why when we talk with people, we don't like to talk of purpose or mission or task. Instead we use the word *focus*, because a focus implies much more the self-choice and changeability that is involved. Like the lens of a camera, you can zoom in and get a wide angle. You can put a filter on it. You can change it altogether, whereas *purpose* sounds as though you have no choice, as though you can do nothing about it, as though on your way into physicalness, someone jotted down something on a piece of paper and said, "Oh, by the way, here's your purpose." It is actually something you deliberately chose to work with in this lifetime, and can subsequently deliberately "un-choose."

Imagine a singular point on a blackboard. That point is now. Originating at that point are hundreds of futures and pasts. Here is now, and out of this now you have any number of futures, any number of them, as many as you can imagine.

One of those futures seems to be thicker, seems to glow and have a sparkle to it. Therefore, when we look at your reality in the now, being able to sense what you have created as the past and what you have created as your future, we will look at it and say, "Well, it looks as if this is what you're going to create." And you can say, "Oh, no, I'm not!" and change it. Or, "Oh, good, good, good!" and keep it up.

That's also why we always tell you why and how to deal with reality. We don't just say, "You're going to get fired in six months." We say, "In the reality you're going to create you're going to get fired in six months. This is why, and this is what you can do about it. Here's a technique you can use to change that reality."

Well, you're open to this idea. You'll admit, "Yeah, I've got lots of probable futures, and it's mine to choose and pick." But you tell yourself, "I only have one past." You have as many pasts as it is possible to have. It's just that this is the one you're telling everybody ... {laughter} ... and you've told this story so long you believe it. ... {laughter} ...

We've been asked upon occasion, "Lazaris, how do I know you're real?" We say back, "How do we know you're real?" ... {laughter} ...

"How can you prove you exist?" Well, you can produce documentation. What? A birth certificate! Oh, come on, we weren't born yesterday. We know about falsification of documents. What are you talking about?

"Here's my passport!" Aha! Who made that up for you, right? ... {laughter} ... How can you prove it?

"Here's my mother!" Sure. How much did you pay her? ... {laughter} ... "No, she really is. She'll promise. She'll take a lie detector test." Ah, sure, you want us to buy that one, eh? What can you do to prove that?

"Well, here's my picture in first grade." Doesn't look very much like you. ... {laughter} ... "Yes, you can see it in the eyes."

No, there is really no way you can prove it absolutely. Your past is an illusion, or possibilities, just as your future is.

Have you ever gone home at Christmas or one of those wonderful gatherings when you run out of things to say in about 20 minutes? ... {laughter} ... And enough of, "How's the job?" Uh-huh. Uh-huh. "And how's the weather been here?" Uh-huh. Uh-huh. "Snowed a lot, eh?" Ummm-hmmm. "Forty degrees and then down to thirty, and the other night it was 23 (yawn) degrees." ... {laughter} ... Running out of things to say and compliments on the wonderful roast, you start reminiscing about the past.

It is fascinating to see how *your* past differs so much from *their* past. Over the years all of you have been busy changing that past that you say is absolute!

Sometimes you dream in your childhood, and that dream becomes a part of that past. You create your own reality, future, present, and past. You choose your destiny, and you decide how much is going to be predetermined. You create it all.

Anonymous Question, Seattle Evening with Lazaris, 1987

Q: Aren't there certain realities that you can't avoid no matter how much you program?

Lazaris: Certainly. There are certain realities that you cannot avoid, but that's not because of the programming. It's because of your belief. Your belief creates thresholds. Your belief is the origin of your reality. If you believe, for example, that if you step out in front of an automobile traveling 60 miles per hour that you're going to get splattered, you can program until you're blue in the face, and you'll still get splattered.

What you would end up having to do is to go in and change the belief. If you change the belief and work with that to a point that you could overcome the threshold — the threshold of that belief that says running out in front of moving automobiles is dangerous to your health — and if you were adequately able to change that, then we would suppose that you could step out in front of a running automobile and not get splattered.

But then the question would be: Why? Why would you waste your time programming something so silly? You can just stay on the sidewalks and avoid it altogether. ... {laughter} ... It makes no sense. It makes absolutely no sense to spend the months, the years, that would be required. Besides that, it's very difficult to test it ... {laughter} ... very difficult to test it. *Splat.* Not there yet ... {laughter} ... What would be the purpose, you see? What would be the purpose?

We've suggested, for example, that you can walk through walls. You can walk through walls. Your scientists tell you that walls are mainly space, and that there's more space in a wall than there is anything solid. And your scientists also tell you that if you could adjust your frequency to vibrate at the same frequency — in other words to vibrate in resonance with the wall — you could then pass right through it.

Well, let's do it, right? ... {laughter} ... Why? Why would you do it? You see, there's a threshold there, a very big threshold there.

As an example, when you are an infant, you learn by observation and routine. You are in the crib, and when you cry mother comes, right? You learn that pretty quickly. And she always comes through that funny space on the wall that's a little different than the rest. You don't know what it's called, but she always seems to come in and out that funny space there. And after a while you learn: DOOR. DOOR is how you get in and out of the room.

So when you finally are old enough to get out of your crib and crawl along the floor you head where? To the wall? ... {laughter} ... You mimic mother, right? You mimic mother, and you go for that funny space on the wall. Not just the wall, but that funny space. And lo and behold it works! You get in and out of the room, and you learn that, and you have a belief, therefore, that when you want to leave a room, you go through the door.

To learn to walk through walls, you have to overcome that threshold in order to resonate at the frequency to walk through them. And again, we'd wonder: Why would you bother?

There are so many more important things to program, and to spend your energy on. There is so much more happening in your life. To waste your time learning to walk through walls is ridiculous. Wait until there are no more doors. ... {laughter} ... When doors are eliminated, then walk through walls. Until then, don't bother.

Anonymous Question, Altanta Evening with Lazaris, 1987

L azaris: All right. That's a confusing point for many people. On the one hand you are going to create the reality, and on the other hand we said it's already done. What's important to understand is that every thought that you have manifests. Absolutely. Every single thought that you have will manifest. Sometimes that manifestation will occur in *this* reality. Those are the ones you enjoy most. But sometimes that manifestation could occur, say, in a past lifetime or in a future lifetime, or it could occur in a parallel lifetime, or it could occur in an Astral expression of yourself.

Let us explain that a little more closely. You've heard the phrase: "Be careful of what you want. You might just get it." Well, we suggest in that similar sense, if you project a thought, if you put it out there, even if you're not trying to program it, even if you're not trying to manifest it necessarily, just put out a thought, a fear, a doubt, a concern, a hope, a wish, a joy — it matters not whether it's positive or negative in your reality — it will manifest. Sometimes as that thought goes out and manifests, it manifests maybe a year from now, maybe 10 years from now, maybe even further down the line in your future. It will manifest.

Q: How would you define creating and manifesting abundance in light of the idea that everything is happening now — that it's already done? In other words, how do you create or manifest something that's already yours?

A person goes around continuously saying, "Ah, it's such a pain in the neck. It's just a pain in the neck. It's such a pain in the neck." That person should not be surprised to create a problem in their neck at some time in their future. Someone who goes around and says it's a pain in some other part of the body might expect to have similar sorts of creations ... {laughter} ... in the reality as well. Somebody who says, "Ach, you'll be the death of me yet — you'll be the death of me yet" just might want to be cautious.

So often you don't remember your thoughts. Thank goodness! You don't consciously record every single thought you have. Therefore, five years from now, ten years from now, when something happens, you don't go, "I thought that back in ... !" Sometimes, though, something happens in your reality and you're moving along and a friend says, "Hey, don't I remember that you were talking about that several years ago, that you were really wanting ..." and you go, "By golly, I was!" Indeed you had forgotten what you had put forth, but it manifested. You forgot. Your reality didn't.

Sometimes those manifestations come in future lifetimes. That's why it's good to be careful what you want. If you are absolutely set on having a huge mansion, and you just absolutely must have that, you might create the potentiality of leaving this lifetime without ever creating it, and then being in the very delicate position of having to come back to a future lifetime just so you can get your mansion, yes? ... {laughter} ... So we suggest that it is wise to be cautious in that regard.

As you project a thought, it can land in your future. It can land in your past. Occasionally, there are those things that occur to you that just seem to come from nowhere. "I don't know where this came from. I didn't even think about it, and here it is, and I have this reality!" We suggest sometimes a future "you" or a past "you" was programming, and you got it. Past lifetimes exist in the same space as yours, but along a continuum of time. Parallel lifetimes are experienced in the same time, but in a different space. Therefore, when you project a thought, it can miss and land in a parallel reality, future, past, or on the Astral plane.

As you are creating, so everything is already done, but you don't always experience it, as you well know. And therefore, as you program something, what you're in essense doing is setting up a resonance and a vibration that will attract that particular reality into this particular reality, so that the two come together as one.

There is a future you who is totally successful, totally happy, has everything you've ever wanted, has that loving relationship, has that wondrous job, has that grand and glorious health. As you program, you set up your resonance field. You create an enticement, if you will, to draw that reality not to land in the future, past, or somewhere else, but into this lifetime, now, so indeed it manifests.

That is how you can program for something that already is. That is how you can create a reality out of nothing and yet at the same time it has already been.

When you go into a movie, for instance, and you sit there, and you're watching it, the end of the movie already exists, does it not? But while you're watching it you forget that, don't you? While you're watching it, ah, you get scared, you get tense, you get all excited, you get all wondering.

For example: You go see a lovely scary movie like "Aliens." Now you know that that's just an actress. That's Sigourney Weaver. That's just a movie. You know that she lives because you saw an interview with her on some talk show three weeks ago. So you know she makes it, and you probably heard from your friends that it ends all right. She wins. It loses. A quick synopsis there.

In the midst of it, however, when the monster's after her, you get just as scared, just as uptight, your adrenalin flows just as hard, you scream just as loud, even though you know it all works out. You're hoping, "Oh, God, I hope she makes it. I hope ..." But you know she does. It's already done! But in the midst of it you don't know that.

Well, you see, if you can get that excited over a two-dimensional reality that's an illusion, how much more excited are you going to get over a three-dimensional reality that you're in the middle of? So although it has already happened, you don't know it. You block it out. In the two-dimensional reality the end is set — it is in the can. In your three-dimensional reality, the ends are there and you get to choose, you get to decide, which one of hundreds of possible and probable ends will be the end. You create ...

You create obstacles physically, emotionally, mentally and intuitively to push the happy endings out of this reality and into another. Therefore, you program and get rid of blockages. You process. You program. You open it up. You create the ambiance, you create the resonance, you do the dance to bring that already existing reality into your creation. That's creating your own reality!

Well, who created it already done? You did. *You did.* Therefore, you're just giving yourself what you have created, and what — we would add — God/Goddess/ All That Is is giving you. So that's how you can manifest and create, even when it's already done.

Anonymous Question, Seattle Evening with Lazaris, 1988

Q: What is the difference between "you do it for me" and allowing help? Is it avoiding responsibility to allow things to come as gifts?

Lazaris: What's the difference? Well, first of all the attitude of "you do it for me" is a manipulation. Allowing help is a function of love. That's perhaps the first difference. Many people expect life to be done for them "just because ... just because I'm here. Just because I exist, you should do it, you should do it for me. I should be given money because I want it. I should be given all the attention because it's owed to me. And you should just do it for me."

As people respond that way, or as you have seen yourself in the past respond that way, you realize what you're really asking for is a manipulation. You want to manipulate. You want other people to create your reality for you. Also, you are not allowing anyone to give to you. Think about it. You go out and buy or stay in and make a gift for a friend. You give it to them. They say, "Thank you. This is owed to me. You were supposed to give me this." How do you feel? The gift is no longer a gift. It is a pseudo-obligation. When you say, "Do it for me," you are denying the opportunity or the possibility of a gift. You are controlling. Denying giving and controlling is what manipulation is.

The bottom-line reason you are physical is to learn to create the reality yourself. That's what you're doing here. Once you learn how, once you understand the method and the methodology of consciously creating that reality, consciously creating success, then a rather interesting paradox occurs. You open up to allowing. You open up to allowing your Higher Self, God/Goddess/All That Is, your Future Self, any number of aspects of yourself to help you create the reality that you desire.

You see, there are teachers in this field who rather will tell you they'll do it for you. "I'll give you this. I'll send you that. I'll make this happen for you. I'll make that happen for you." First, that's not true, because you create your own reality, not they. Second, such statements are prime ways to take away your power, to remove your power from you. "I will make your life happy" is a way to rob you of that experience and rob you of that power.

There are certain points in your evolution where you do let it be done for you, because you have not yet learned how to do it yourself. But now is the time in your Age, now is the time in your humanity and in your world where it is for you to create it for yourself. One of the paradoxes is that once you have done that, once you have demonstrated your creative ability to yourself, once you've shown yourself and convinced yourself adequately that you do know how to consciously create your success, then — without manipulation — you can allow it to come in.

What are you allowing? What you want. You see, "you do it for me" is different than saying, "I can create it, and, together with my Unseen Friends, I'm going to allow it to come into my reality. I've done my processing. I've done my programming. I know what I want and why I want it. I've handled all of that and now — after creating the ambiance — I'm going to allow it to occur."

That, we suggest, is an act of receiving as opposed to an act of manipulation. Is it lacking responsibility — is it neglecting responsibility — to allow? No. To expect it to be done for you is an act of manipulation and control. To allow it to be done is an act of love — an act of receiving love.

Anonymous Question, Seattle Evening with Lazaris, 1988

To Conclude ...

Lazaris: We know there are those who suggest: "No, you can't be responsible for anything but your own little lonesome self." And that is sad. It is so limiting to think in those terms. There is a grander world for which you can at least take a piece of responsibility. With a piece of responsibility comes a piece of power, and with a greater piece of responsibility comes a greater piece of power. As you are willing to be more and more responsible in your own quite unique and personal way, so you will become more and more powerful. You will be able to take stock of your world and treat it as the community it is and make those decisions. The world can be a safe place.

Again, there are those who will talk of problems. But start looking for solutions, not in the old way, not in the linear scope that you've always looked. You have always begun at the beginning and found some logic. Now look in an exponential way, reaching for the fact that: "There is a solution, and my job is the curious one of discovering it." As you will see your world as a global community for which you are partly, and more so, increasingly responsible — and as you will see the problems that seem unsolvable as intricate problems to which solutions have not yet been considered — as you know there will be solutions even though you don't know what they are yet — then you can feel that you have chosen to have the world be a more positive and loving place. And you can be increasingly responsible and say to yourself, "I was partly responsible for this piece of the world — for this wonder in the world."

Q: Is there a concluding comment that you would like to leave us with?

You know, many years ago, very many years ago, Magellan sailed around South America, and when he landed his big, big ships (they had huge, masted ships, three-masted ships), the natives couldn't see them. The natives couldn't see those ships, because they were beyond their conception, beyond anything they could perceive. Those ships were moored in a sea of impossibility.

"Now I am beginning to see a world of love, light, laughter and joy!"

Oh, clearly they could see the small boats the Spanish came to shore upon, because they were similar to their own canoes — strange, but nonetheless similar! But they couldn't see the big ships, and as they looked out on the sea they saw an unbroken horizon. There was nothing upon it, until the teachers came — until the spiritual teachers came along and said, "Look it's out there along that horizon. Look for something that's about 'yeh' long and about 'yeh' high that has this and this and, oh, some of that." The natives looked, and they looked, and they strained.

Now this is not conjecture: This is a fact of history from Magellan's own writings as he had talked of the phenomenon.

They looked and looked. Finally one or two would say: "Does it have a red flag hanging?"

"Oh, yes, you're starting to see it! You're starting to see it!"

Well, in that same sense, you're in a world now where when you look out on that horizon, it looks unbroken. It looks like there is no hope, and there's no change. Your world is getting worse and worse every day, with all the things that are going wrong. It's just an unbroken horizon of abysmalness. And we want to come along and say, "It's beautiful out there. There's fun to be had. There's success to be created. There's joy to be experienced, and there's life to be celebrated."

And you say, "Lazaris, I just can't see it. I just can't see it. All I see is Doom and Gloom, misery and pain." And that's OK. We'll keep pointing. "Look this way, look like that, and try to shift your attitude over here. If you look at the world a little bit differently ..."

And then one, and then another, and then another, and soon many more of you start to see: "By golly, I do see a world that can be different than all that is being predicted. I do see a world that can be filled with love, filled with happiness. I do see a world in which I can celebrate the wonder of life, rather than being afraid of the disaster. Before I could only see a world of hate, darkness, pain and despair. Now I am beginning to see a world of love, light, laughter and joy."

One, then another, then another, and soon ... you.

Merv Griffin, **The Merv Griffin Show***, July, 1986*

With love and peace ...

Lazaris

Appendix

More Information about Lazaris ...

Lazaris regularly conducts evening, one-day and weekend workshops (and sometimes seminars that are four days or longer) on an ever-expanding variety of topics. You will find a description of some of these on the next page. Lazaris visits many major American cities each year. A partial list of those cities includes Los Angeles, San Francisco, Atlanta, New Orleans, Seattle, Houston, Miami, Boston, Chicago, Philadelphia & Tampa.

Private consultations with Lazaris are available, though they cannot be guaranteed due to the number of people requesting them. If you would like to request a reading, please write to Concept: Synergy at the address below and ask us to send you a "Consultation Request Form."

If you would like to be placed on Lazaris' mailing list and be notified of workshops and seminars, please call or write us at:

Concept: Synergy, 279 S. Beverly Drive, Suite 604
Beverly Hills, CA 90212
213/285-1507 or 714/337-0789.

Lazaris Seminars

Since October, 1974, when Lazaris began channeling through, he has been constantly and consistently working with people to help them regain their personal power and to guide and befriend them on their Spiritual Journey Home. He has, over the last 14 years, given thousands of personal consultations, and produced dozens of magnificent audio and video tapes (see the following pages for a list of tapes). He also provides an incredibly special experience of growth, empowerment and love through the numerous seminars he conducts.

Evenings with Lazaris are monthly seminars given in Los Angeles and San Francisco, and once or twice a year in various other cities across the United States. Each month the topic is different as Lazaris continues to unfold the pathway to greater personal freedom and deeper personal spirituality. Over the years, Lazaris has covered an amazing array of topics, giving both understanding of how to deal with aspects of personal growth and techniques to move forward into ever-increasing levels of self-love and personal power. Many of these are available now on tape. Each Evening with Lazaris is 3-1/2 hours long and will include both a meditation and a Blending. The taped versions include all of the material of the Evenings except the Blendings.

Weekends with Lazaris have been described as "quantum leap" experiences. They are deeply enriching and enabling, a time to move powerfully forward in growth and to gain a far deeper experience of our true selves, our Unseen Friends, our Higher Self, and God/Goddess/All That Is. The information given by Lazaris is profound, and there are always several very deep meditations. Sometimes Weekends with Lazaris incorporate a One-Day Workshop with Lazaris. The Weekends and One-Days are recorded for copyrighting purposes; however, the tapes have not been released for sale.

Longer Seminars with Lazaris. Over the past several years Lazaris has done several workshops that have been from four to five days long. The first of these was **Realizing Lemuria**, a five-day seminar which was available in 1987. **The Intensive** is a series of seminars, each with a different topic, that are available in 1988 in June, August and October. They are from two to four days long, depending upon the seminar. The Intensive may or may not be available in future years.

For complete information on Lazaris seminars, please contact Concept: Synergy (213/285-1507). We will be glad to provide you with a full list of workshops and seminars.

Channel Jach Pursel ...

Jach Pursel, Lazaris' only channel, was born and raised in Michigan and was graduated from the University of Michigan with a degree in political science in 1969. When Lazaris came through in 1974, Jach was living in Florida and was, as he says, "climbing the corporate ladder," pursuing a career as a business executive for a national company.

Jach Pursel now spends about 30 hours per week channeling Lazaris for private consultations as well as seminars and workshops. In addition, he is Vice President of Isis Rising and Illuminarium Gallery (art galleries), Visionary Publishing, Inc., (an art publishing company) and FutureVision (an investment company). He resides in Beverly Hills, where Isis Rising is located at One Rodeo Drive.

Lazaris VideoTapes

Each of these Lazaris videos is available in VHS, Beta, and PAL. Each tape is two hours long. Cost: $59.95 plus shipping and sales tax if you live in California. There are order forms on the last pages of this book.

Awakening the Love
This tape includes an introduction to Lazaris. Lazaris beautifully and clearly explores "What is Love" and "How to Love Yourself More."

Forgiving Yourself
Spiritual growth begins with self-love and self-forgiveness. Lazaris examines these integral components of The Journey Home.

The Secrets of Manifesting What You Want I
Lazaris discusses several specific programming techniques, including his "33-Second Technique." In meditation we journey to the Causal Plane where programming is intensified.

The Secrets of Manifesting What You Want II
Lazaris moves beyond the necessary tools and materials of creation into the wondrous mysteries and secrets that underlie creating your own reality. Two 33-Second Techniques are included in the final meditation.

Personal Power & Beyond ...
Lazaris explores the core ingredients of Personal Power. Beyond lies the wondrous World of Dominion.

Achieving Intimacy & Loving Relationships
How to create and expand intimacy; how to discover and increase all kinds of loving relationships (not only romantic ones).

Unconditional Love
How to honestly unfold the beauty and the power of the love that is unconditional. Includes a guided meditation.

Releasing Negative Ego
How to distinguish between positive and negative ego. How to elegantly release the negative ego while you develop a positive ego. Includes a transformative meditation.

Unlocking the Power of Changing Your Life
Goes beyond Manifesting What You Want to changing what you already have. Includes the Power of Choice, Power of Image, and a fantastic Change Process.

Spiritual Mastery: The Journey Begins
An exhilarating exploration of each step of our Spiritual Journey. Includes a powerful guided meditation.

Personal Excellence
An in-depth exploration of elegance and excellence — a fundamental step in the Journey Home. Concludes with a powerful meditation.

Developing a Relationship with Your Higher Self
Discover the love between you and your Higher Self. With a magnificent meditation.

The Mysteries of Empowerment
Through discussion and meditation gain the permission and authority to be powerful. Empowerment is a profound mystery of spiritual growth.

The Future: How To Create It
The future: It is filled either with the darkness of fear and inevitabilities or with the shimmer of love and possibilities. Discover how to create the future you want. Includes a beautiful meditation.

Overcoming Fear of Success
More than ever we are ready to deal directly with our fear of succeeding. Lazaris offers liberating understanding and technique.

Developing Self-Confidence
In this tape Lazaris deals with Self-Confidence from a personal and global viewpoint. The whole world is watching and waiting for us to rebuild — to heal — confidence.

Listening to the Whispers
If you listen to the whispers, you don't have to hear the shouts. A fascinating discussion of how to use your reality as gentle feedback for your evaluation.

Personal Growth Tapes

The following are 2-hour cassettes with meditations and are taken from the Evenings with Lazaris over the past few years. Cost of each is $24.95 plus shipping and handling, and sales tax for California residents.

Healing: The Nature of Health I
Healing: The Nature of Health II
The Secrets of Spirituality I
The Secrets of Spirituality II
Loving
Being Loved
Crystals: The Power & Use
Busting & Building Ego
Programming What You Want
The Crisis of Martyrhood
Intimacy
The Magick of Relationships
Earth Energy/Earth Power
The Unseen Friends
Busting & Building Image
Consciously Creating Success
Responsibility & Freedom
Excellence
The Tapestry of Success
The Power of Dominion
Positive Ambition
Gratitude
The Mysterious Power of Chakras
Ending Guilt

The Secrets of Manifesting What
   You Want I
Fear: The Internal War
Discovering Your Subconscious
With Love & Peace
Developing Self-Confidence
Conquering Fear
Ending Self-Punishment
Ending Self-Sabotage
Harmony: The Power Vortex
Freedom: Its Mystery & Power
Balance: Releasing the Full Self
Abundance: The Skill
The Elegance of Abundance
A Private Consultation
Inner Peace
Harmonic Convergence: The Ritual
   of Emergence
1988: The Year of Compassion
Lazaris Talks about AIDS at the
   Hay House
Self-Esteem
Self-Worth & Self-Respect
I Deserve!

Books

The Sacred Journey: You and Your Higher Self

The Higher Self ... to reach it, to touch it, to have it touch back has been the dream of spiritual seekers for millenia ... Lazaris lays out a path that leads to the Higher Self, a path of certainty and confidence and preparation that leads to the experience that when you touch your Higher Self, and it touches back, it is real ... $9.95 plus shipping/handling (and sales tax for California residents)

Lazaris Interviews: Book II

Beautiful and elucidating answers to questions on death, reincarnation, emotional and spiritual growth, more esoteric subjects like kundalini and power points, and questions about Lazaris himself. $9.95 plus shipping/handling (and sales tax for California residents).

Lazaris Audio Cassette Tapes

Lazaris Discussions

On Releasing Anger/On Releasing Self-Pity $29.95
On Releasing Guilt/On Receiving Love $29.95
Healing & Releasing Hurt/The Keys of Happiness $29.95

The Red Label Series (Meditations) $29.95 each.

Reducing Fear & Worry/Reducing Stress
Self-Confidence/Self-Awareness
High Energy/Enthusiasm
Happiness/Peace
Reduced Sleep/Improved Sleep
Personal Power/Power & Dominion
Productivity/Impeccability
Improved Health/Balance & Harmony

Other Meditations

Cleaning Chakras/Pituitary-Pineal Meditation $19.95
Beyond the Threshold/Editing the Film $19.95
The Goddess Series I $29.95
The Goddess Series II $29.95
Handling Menstruation $29.95

Lazaris & Peny Tapes $14.95

April 1986 Evening with Lazaris & Peny
July 1986 Evening with Lazaris & Peny
November 1986 Evening with Lazaris & Peny
San Francisco March 1987 Evening with Lazaris & Peny
Los Angeles March 1987 Evening with Lazaris & Peny

Lazaris - Gilbert Williams Calendars $14.95

"For as long as there is Light,
we will love you..."

— *Lazaris*

LAZARIS TAPES
ORDER FORM

_____

NAME

_____

ADDRESS

_____

CITY - STATE - ZIP

_____

PHONE #

☐ PLEASE ADD MY NAME TO THE MAILING LIST:

Qty.	Tape Title	Price

VISA, MASTERCARD, AMEX, Accepted

_____

Charge Card Number-Exp. Date

_____

Signature

Money Order &
Charge Card orders
shipped within 1 week,
CA checks held 7 days
out-of-state checks held
21 days

*10.00 charge for
returned checks*

SUBTOTAL	
6.5% Tax CA Res.	
5% Postage 15% overseas	
($1.00 Minimum) TOTAL	

CONCEPT: SYNERGY

213/285-1500

LAZARIS INTERVIEWS, BOOK I

279 S. Beverly Dr.
Suite 604
Beverly Hills, CA 90212